The goal of the mystical life is for us to become beholders of God in action, where we ascribe nothing to ourselves—not even good motives. We no longer have desires. We no longer have needs. . . . This is called "living by Grace." . . . If I prayed for something, it would mean I have a desire, an end, an object in life that I am seeking. But I have nothing to pray for. I have only this minute to live, this minute in which I must be fulfilled by the Spirit. . . . That is what the mystical life is—attaining that degree where every day you find yourself not wondering about tomorrow because there is no tomorrow for you; there is only a tomorrow for God.

Living by Grace

OTHER BOOKS BY JOEL S. GOLDSMITH

The Art of Meditation
Practicing the Presence
The Thunder of Silence
The Art of Spiritual Healing
A Parenthesis in Eternity
Living the Infinite Way
The Mystical I
Our Spiritual Resources
Joel Goldsmith's Gift of Love
Invisible Supply

Living by Grace

The Path to Inner Discovery

JOEL S. GOLDSMITH

HarperSanFrancisco
A Division of HarperCollins*Publishers*

All quotations from the Bible are taken from the King James Version.

LIVING BY GRACE: *The Path to Inner Discovery.* Copyright © 1984, 1992 by Geri McDonald, Executrix of The Estate of Joel S. Goldsmith. All rights reserved. Printed in the United States of America. No part of this book may be used or reproduced in any manner whatsoever without written permission except in the case of brief quotations embodied in critical articles and reviews. For information address HarperCollins Publishers, 10 East 53rd Street, New York, NY 10022.

FIRST HARPERCOLLINS PAPERBACK EDITION PUBLISHED IN 1994
ISBN 0-06-250316-2 (pbk)
An Earlier Edition of This Book Was Cataloged As Follows:
Goldsmith, Joel S.
Living by grace: the path to inner unfoldment / Joel S.
Goldsmith.—1st ed.
p. cm.
ISBN 0-06-250538-6 (alk. paper)
1. Spiritual life. 2. Mysticism. I. Title.
BV5082.2G63 1992   91-58164
248.4—dc20   CIP

94 95 96 97 98 ❖ HAD 10 9 8 7 6 5 4 3 2 1

This edition is printed on acid-free paper that meets the American National Standards Institute Z39.48 Standard.

Except the Lord build the house, they
labor in vain that build it.

—PSALM 127

Illumination dissolves all material ties and binds men together with
the golden chains of spiritual understanding; it acknowledges only
the leadership of the Christ; it has no ritual or rule but the divine,
impersonal universal Love; no other worship than the inner Flame
that is ever lit at the shrine of Spirit. This union is the free state
of spiritual brotherhood. The only restraint is the discipline
of Soul, therefore we know liberty without license; we are
a united universe without physical limits; a divine
service to God without ceremony or creed.
The illumined walk without fear—by Grace.

—THE INFINITE WAY

CONTENTS

Living by Grace

CHAPTER 1

THE SECRET OF SUCCESS

Spiritual completeness and perfection are the gift of God. This gift was given to each of us at the time we were created—from the very beginning. Everyone has this gift, because God is no respecter of persons. He never chose one person to have more spirituality than another nor made one individual better or more spiritual than another. The message of The Infinite Way was not revealed to me because I am a special child of God. The Father gave me no monopoly on His blessings or on His Grace. I do not have any monopoly on God at all! The message of The Infinite Way was revealed to me so that I could reveal it to you; then you in turn can go out and demonstrate and then reveal it to others. But you cannot teach it if you have not learned it and demonstrated it yourself!

Every one of us has the same seed of God—the same Divinity, the same spiritual impulse. That is one thing we have in common. While it is true that the Master was speaking to the Hebrews when He taught, "The Kingdom of God is in you," one can hardly believe that He meant only the Hebrews had it. It would be a tragic world if that were so! When the Master spoke those words, the Hebrews were the only ones physically

1

present, but He was not talking to them exclusively; He was imparting the universal spiritual Word of life.

When the Disciple said, "Thou hast the Word of God," and "The Kingdom of God is within you," and when he spoke of "your Father" and "my Father," he was not speaking only to the Hebrews but to all of mankind! Paul recognized this and then Peter, and they went out into the world and preached the Word to the gentiles, the pagans, and anyone who would listen to them. Eventually everyone in the world had this Word preached to them. The Word was to be spoken to all of mankind, everywhere, and under every condition—even to sinners—for we are all equal in God, we are all children of God, we are one in Divine sonship. That never changes, even though we may temporarily forget it when we are unhappy, ill, or poor!

Know that the Spirit of God indwells you, then go on to know what Its function is which is to heal you and others, to re-form and forgive you and others, to feed the hungry, and to resurrect the dead. You will be called on to "go forth and do likewise," because once you have entered this path, you cannot turn back without turning into "a pillar of salt." Once you have seen this vision, you have to go forward even if you have some hard experiences before you demonstrate the principles. I had some tough ones to go through, and I know that they cannot be avoided. The spiritual path is not easy; it is straight and narrow, and few there be that enter!

Again, you cannot teach the message of The Infinite Way until you have learned the principles and then demonstrated them. That will be our method of study from now on: taking the principles and working with them. One by one, the principles will come alive for you when you read about them in books or hear about them on tape recordings. Eventually you will be able to say, "Whereas before I was blind, now I can see what the Master meant, what the ancient Hebrew prophets knew, what modern mystical teachers are revealing." When you can truthfully say this, you will have proven that you have the secret of life.

The Principle of Supply

Let us take up the matter of supply first, because the principle applies whether it is supply of income or funds, supply of health, supply of companionship, or supply of happiness. For now, we will take it from the standpoint of supply as money, income, abundance—whatever we want to call it.

In older orthodox teachings, we were led to believe that supply was something outside of ourselves and that we could go to God, ask for it, beg for it, and it would be given to us. If you have been doing that long enough, you must know that it does not work! If one could just ask God for supply and get it, there would not be so many poor people on earth and there would not be so many people relying on the government. You can be assured that if people could go to God for supply, they would not be relying on the government!

Then came the metaphysical era, which perpetuated this false teaching that you could demonstrate supply; that is, that you could get supply or have supply brought to you. That has not worked very well either, because the movements that were founded on that belief have not obtained enough supply to keep them going. We therefore know that there is really no way to get supply or to demonstrate supply. We must look further for another principle.

The harmony of your being is already stored within you, and you have only to bring it forth from within you into fullness of expression, not try to add it to yourself from the outside. The principle of supply revealed to me through the Bible is that you can demonstrate an infinity of supply—if you do it in accordance with what the Bible teaches us. Let us start with Elijah and work up to Jesus.

Elijah was a man of God, a great Hebrew prophet, who had already demonstrated that when he needed food, ravens would bring it to him if there was no other way for it to reach him. Or, he could wake up and find cakes baked on a stone right in front of him. No human hand did this for him!

Then we find Elijah meeting a widow who was so poor that her son was about to be taken in slavery in payment of her debts. She appealed to Elijah, the man of great wisdom, to save her son. Although Elijah knew how poor she was, he asked her, "What have you in the house?" She replied, "A few drops of oil and a handful of meal." Elijah instructed her to bake the last bit of meal and oil that she had in the house and give him the cakes. Now, asking an extremely poor person to give you the last bit of food in the house is about as cruel and heartless as you would expect to hear from a man of wisdom! However, Elijah was not being heartless. He was trying to teach a lesson, and he succeeded because the widow, knowing that Elijah was a dedicated, consecrated spiritual teacher, obeyed him. Had she not been obedient, the lesson would never have been learned. She began to pour the oil from the cruse, and it never stopped pouring until all her needs and that of her son and Elijah were met. Where, then, did her supply come from? It came from within herself, and she demonstrated her supply by her willingness to share her last morsel.

Our supply is like a spider's web. It comes from within our own being where the Kingdom of God is. Nothing more can be added to us. All that is required is that we "prime the pump" by letting some little thing flow from us. But you must share *without* the expectation of a return, without any "bargaining" about it. Sharing with your family or friends, from whom you could expect a return, is not sharing! It is a form of bargaining! Most people have no trouble sharing with their wives or husbands, with their children, or with their parents. It is a little more difficult to give to their neighbor's children—those down the street or those in Africa, China, Japan, or elsewhere. We are all bottled up in ourselves and our own families, and we let others take care of themselves and their own families, forgetting that we are supposed to love our neighbors as ourselves.

To demonstrate supply, then, we must first ask ourselves not who will give to us or what is there for us to get, but, "What do I have in the house that I can begin to pour, to share?" Somewhere within ourselves we have to find a few drops of oil, or a little meal, or an old pair of shoes, or a few pennies in our purses. We must find something that we can give, pour, share.

Money, food, clothing are not the only things we have stored within us which we can give of in order to start the flow from within us. We can find some forgiveness for someone or perform some service for someone. When you are serving man, you are serving God. The Master said, "Inasmuch as ye have done it unto the least of these my brethren, ye have done it unto me." You are not serving God unless you are serving man, including the very least of them. The only way you can serve God is by your service to mankind—not only to the rich, the handsome, and the beautiful but to the very least of them. The only way we have of serving God is by serving our fellowman, whether it is the sharing of dollars, pounds, or pennies or the forgiving or praying for our enemies. Scripture tells us that if you say you love God and do not love your fellowman, you are a liar!

Forgive and Pray for Enemies

We could forgive our enemies—pray to God to forgive those who have offended us, insulted us, and grievously used us. Forgive not only those who have personally injured us but also those who have hurt our nation, our race, our religion, our friends, our relatives. Forgive those who have hurt mankind in general, those who have held others in bondage. We could pray to God to forgive those who are in prison and give them a new mind.

We could pray for our enemies. Jesus Christ tells us that it profits us nothing to pray for our friends and that we must pray for our enemies as well. Yet, during the two world wars, do you know how few churches held services exclusively to pray for the enemy? Let us spend two minutes a day forgiving our enemies and praying, "Forgive them, Father, they know not what they do," whether they are personal enemies, enemies of our nation, or just enemies of mankind, or any other kind of enemy. If we accept Christ Jesus as our Master, Teacher, Spiritual Guide, we must obey His teachings. Then we become children of God, joint heirs with Christ to all of the heavenly riches. Doing otherwise is trying to demonstrate supply or health in opposition to His teachings.

There is no spiritual power quite as great as that which comes from forgiving and praying for the enemy. Forgiving our enemies and praying for them generates great spiritual power because it is Love. What we do for friends and neighbors is only a personal sense of love—not Love—and therefore has no spiritual power. Spiritual power is in Love for our fellowman, whether he is friend or foe, white or black, saint or sinner—the kind of Love that says, "Neither do I condemn thee; go and sin no more. Thy sins be forgiven thee."

To enjoy the fruitage of an abundant supply, give up all desire and struggle for it. Just start living spiritually by giving, pouring, forgiving. Once will not do any good, twice will not do any good, three times will not do any good. Forgive seventy times seven. Whatever you pour out—even if it is only a few pennies—will continue to pour without ceasing, and the pennies will grow into dollars.

Most people dam up their flow of supply by trying to keep too much of yesterday's manna instead of putting it to use. I have watched this for thirty years. We dam up our supply

because we do not give, pour, forgive, and pray for our enemies.
You can see how this works in nature. Take for instance a rose
bush. If you do not remove the roses, soon there is no room for
more to bloom. You have choked off your supply of roses! But
the more roses you remove, the more will grow. It is the same
with fruit on a tree. If you leave a crop of oranges on the tree,
how will you get another crop next year? Of course, nature will
take care of it by letting them drop off, but that is a waste. You
may as well pluck them off and give them away rather than
choking off your supply.

Another way we choke off our supply is by trying to get
more than we have. You do not get anything from this world
that you do not first put in the world—whether it is good or
evil. The bread that you cast on the water is the bread that
comes back to you. Any bread cast on the water by someone
else cannot come back to you. If you reach out and try to grab
it, your fingers will get burned. For example, the bread that I
have cast on the water comes back to me, and that leaves none
for you. The only supply you get is from the bread you have cast
on the water; you are entitled to none other. That lesson is
taught throughout Scripture. That is why we are taught,
"Whatsoever things that you would have happen to you, do ye
that to the others." Why? You are setting in motion that which
is coming back to you. The evil that comes back to us may also
be caused by our ignorance of the Truth. "Ye shall know the
Truth, and the Truth shall set you free." You cannot be made
free if you do not know the Truth; and you are therefore in
bondage. It may be the bondage of lack of supply, the bondage
of ill health, the bondage of sin, or the bondage of false ap-
petite. If you know the Truth, if you live the Truth, and if you
obey the Truth, then you are made free of such bondage. Know
the Truth that "the Father and I are one, and all that the Father
has is mine," and then begin to share it instead of trying to get
more than you have! That is The Infinite Way principle of supply: giving, pouring, sharing.

When we give, share, and pour, we do not make a public display because the Father rewards us openly only for what we do in secrecy. It is true that you can get a lot of credit from your neighbors by being seen going to church or being seen putting money in the collection plate. But you lose the reward from the Father who seeth in secrecy and rewards openly. By giving, sharing, and pouring—and doing so secretly—we have the whole secret of supply.

We need not seek for what we shall eat or what we shall drink. This does not mean that we shall not work, but that we are not working for a living. We instead are working as part of our fulfillment. Our supply does not always come from what we are doing for a living. It does not always come through those we benefit most. But then, it is not up to us to designate who shall give to us or how much. Our function is to serve to the best of our ability and let the supply come from whence it will. Our thought is never to be on when our supply will come or how much or how little it will be, but on how much we can do, how well we can do it, and how much we keep pouring. We are responsible only for sharing what we already have. We have all of our supply within us.

From the Letter of Truth to the Spirit of Truth

Since God constitutes our individual being, all that the Father has is ours. Therefore we do not hope to get anything more from God or from man. The Infinite Way does not teach that God will do certain things for you or bring certain blessings to you or that you can achieve something for yourself. We are the servants of God, and there is no room for profit or self-glorification. There can be no personal glory in sharing Truth, because the revealed Truth is God's, not yours or mine.

If you are touched by the Spirit of God and wish to share it, you must never lose sight of the fact that what you are sharing is God's Grace pouring through you. Just as you have received it freely from God, so must you give freely of what has come through God. If there is to be a return (a reward), it will be a reflex action of what you have given.

The idea of sharing comes to different people in different ways. The idea of sharing came to me at first in healing work. Later, the idea of sharing was exemplified in the writing of books. Still later, it was by teaching. But these activities were not for my profit; they were just ways of sharing what had come to me. As a result of these activities, there was enough supply for my living and for my family's and for my travels. But if I had gone into these activities for that purpose, they would have failed!

There was never any idea in my mind that I would at any time ever be connected with religious, philosophical, or metaphysical work. That was no part of my consciousness. As far as I was concerned, I was a businessman, and except for some momentary periods that everyone sooner or later has in business, I was not doing too badly. At best, I had a hunger to find something more satisfying than a highball or a card game, the theater or a dance, or even a successful business. I was trying to find something better.

Most of us come to our Grace of God through our ills or discords. Mine came through illness. I was very ill with a severe cold that I could not rise above. One Saturday I sought out a practitioner whom I had never heard of previously and who usually did not see patients on Saturdays, when he devoted his time to study and prayer. But when he saw the condition I was in, he invited me into his office. Not only did I have an instantaneous healing, but also after leaving his office, I could not smoke or drink, or play cards anymore.

Two days later, someone asked me for a healing, and got it. The next day someone else came to me and asked, "Will you pray for me?" and had a healing. This went on for a year and a half. By then I was in the practice of healing. That had not been my intent; I was not seeking it. It just came upon me. For sixteen years I was in healing work. I was very happy in it, very successful in it, and very prosperous in it. I had no reason to give it up, and I would have been happy to stay in it sixteen or thirty more years.

Then a series of experiences and unfoldments came to me that resulted in my writing the book *The Infinite Way* (Marina del Rey, Ca.: Devorss). Only two thousand copies were printed, and I felt that only a few hundred would be sold to some of my friends and patients. I never dreamed of anything beyond that. I expected to go on with my healing work. If any of my patients wanted to know more, a copy of *The Infinite Way* could be had at that time for $2.00 a copy.

It did not happen that way. I was invited to speak at a Unity Center in Los Angeles. I talked there for seven weeks. I thought it was just an incident that would not happen again. But then I was invited to speak at a metaphysical library in San Francisco. There I was asked to give a class. Although I had had groups who came regularly to my office in Los Angeles, I had never thought of giving a class. Now the San Francisco group wanted a class. So my very first closed class was held in San Francisco. One step after another led to the present activities of The Infinite Way. None of this was planned. I never once had the idea of going into such an activity. I was simply led into each step. Never once was there any thought of gain or profit. The activities were just a way for me to share.

The activity of God operates in human consciousness. It goes through our consciousness and calls us to do the work. We do not do it; we do not plan it that way. The activity of God simply operates through our consciousness. We are only the instruments through which God's activity takes place, so there can be no personal glory in it.

In order for the great Self (the Spirit) to become greater in our experience, the little self must die daily. That is taught by all spiritual or mystical teachers and writers. Paul says that our self must die daily so that we can be reborn of the Spirit. The Master's teaching guarantees the destruction of your little self and ensures the rebirth of your real Self, the I that I am. He tells us there are two things we must not do in public: we must not pray where man can see us, and we must not do our alms and benevolences where man can see us.

If the world can point to you and say how generous you are or how holy you are because you carry around a Bible or have not missed church in twenty years, that inflates the self. That gives glory to you and in that degree cheats you of a God-experience. When you can deflate your human selfhood by not putting it on parade or setting it up in public or getting a reputation for this or that, when you are not seeking praise for your charitableness or your mercifulness or benevolence, then you permit the I that I am to perform Its work, and the Presence and Power of God in the invisible appears visibly and tangibly in this world.

The same principle applies to a metaphysical or spiritual treatment or prayer. Any treatment or prayer that is a silent realization or recognition of God appears visibly as the health of somebody else.

If you can grasp that principle, you will understand why success can come only when there is no desire for success. When you have caught a glimpse of this Truth or, by the Grace of God, have been given a little healing or teaching gift and are willing to share it without any thought of saving anybody or saving yourself or supplying anybody or yourself, then out of that sharing comes such activity as you have seen in The Infinite Way. If you can grasp this principle of sharing, you will understand why success can come only when an individual has no desire for success, no desire to save the world or to heal the world or teach the world. That is the secret that will ensure success in any activity in which you may be engaged, and the success will come because of the activity of Truth in your consciousness. You will not have to advertise, and you will not have to tell anyone that you are following a spiritual path or that you believe in God. You will never have to open your lips of your own accord, because this principle absolutely sets aside any sense of self that might interfere with your demonstration of the activity of God in your consciousness.

CHAPTER 2

RISING INTO SPIRITUAL CONSCIOUSNESS

In our work we do not ask for loyal followers. Certainly I do not want any personal followers, and I am sure that those who get anywhere in this work will never want personal followers. Our only desire must be to share with others whatever God-given Grace we have so that they can find God too. But no one will ever find God by merely following a particular teaching and obeying its rules and regulations. You find God through the study of the letter of Truth combined with meditation, prayer, and a very humble desire to know God, "whom to know aright is life eternal."

There have been Catholic mystics, Protestant mystics, Christian Science mystics, Unity mystics, and New Thought mystics who knew God aright. In any one of their teachings, there is enough Truth and light to lead you to the Kingdom of God although there are many errors in them. It makes no difference whether you are an Infinite Way student, a Christian Scientist, or some other. You will achieve results even if you are following a teaching that is not entirely correct in its statements of Truth as long as you are not merely concerned about glorifying the teaching. Any teaching must be considered only

13

as an aid in your search for the light of revelation. Do not follow a teaching just to be thought of as some kind of loyal fol-
lower of the teaching or of the teacher. All you have to be
concerned with is knowing God aright and with your relationship with God, and staying with it through the trials and tribu-
lations until it brings you to the spiritual experience of
knowing God.

When that experience takes place, you will lose all anxi-
ety and fear for yourself. Fear and responsibility will drop away.
Your supply will begin to flow without your taking thought for
your life. You will no longer have to support yourself by physical or mental means. You will know that you are the same infinite spiritual being that you now are no matter whether you are
sick or well, or dead or alive. You will not worry about whether
you live on one plane of consciousness or on another. You will
know that your health is being taken care of as if there really
were a God who cared, because by that time you will have
come into actual experience of God-caring. You will no longer
try to establish health by thought processes or knowing-the-
truth processes.

At this point, you must guard against two things. The first
one is becoming concerned for the members of your family who
do not know the Truth and wanting to bring them right into
heaven with you. You must overcome that complex very
quickly and let them work out their own salvation. They will
come up either through Grace or through difficulties as you did.
By trying to save them from their difficulties, you are more apt
to be dragged down to their level than you are apt to take them
up with you.

The second thing you must guard against is wanting to give
the Truth to the world. Let us not be all "puffed up" with the
idea that we have something with which to save the world,
because we do not. It has been my experience that I cannot
save even one individual. I can truthfully say that in twenty-
five years of my work, I do not know of one single soul that I

have saved. Not one! I have seen some who have come to their own realization and demonstration of God, but they did it themselves because they were longing for it, they were looking for it, they were exposing themselves to it. But I did not do it; they did. All we can do is bring about our own delivery from bondage to human sense. Then when we have achieved it, those who are open and receptive and responsive can come to us and receive a bit of the light that is shining through us. But first they must claim it for their own and demonstrate it.

So do not get the idea that now that you have the light you can go out to save the world, your relatives, or friends. Keep your spiritual light secret and sacred. When others discern it, share it with them but only to the extent of their capacity to receive it. Otherwise, keep it secret and sacred.

I am not trying to save the world. I am not carrying the gospel anywhere. Since my work began, I have never gone any place until I was invited. In some cases, I have not gone until I received repeated invitations. I am not advertising in newspapers or magazines. When I receive an invitation, if the inner guidance says, "Yes, go!" I go. Otherwise, I stay at home and live by my own conscious realization of God. Then when an individual or a group comes to me, I share it with them. But I never go anywhere with the intention of saving anyone or carrying anyone to heaven with me or healing anyone. When I am invited, it is my joy to go and share, but never with the intention of "selling" or giving the light. You came here to receive it. That is the difference.

I never offer it to my sister or brother because they have not reached out for it or asked for it or desired it. Occasionally they ask for a healing, and they get it. As far as I am concerned, that is as much as they want, so that is as much as they get. But when one of them says to me, "Now I am ready; now I want it," I am ready to share it, but not one minute before! So whether it is my brother or my sister or you in this class or all of you who are out in the world, it is not my function to convert you or save you or to mind your business. My function is to mind my own business, to go away for forty days—or four hundred days—and live by communion with God. Then if you should say to me, "Give me some of that meat, that drink, that wine, that water, that spiritual food," you will find that I will respond to that call, and I will share the light with you insofar as I have received it. From there on, you have to take it and work with it even if at first it is on an intellectual plane only. The time will come when it passes from an intellectual agreement to a spiritual experience.

When your spiritual experience comes, it will not be long before you are called upon for healings or instruction or guidance. Then it will be your function to answer. But do not say, "Go and see my practitioner." When the call is made upon you, God's grace will give you the wisdom and the healing power to respond to the call. Do not say, "Here is a book" or "Here is my practitioner's telephone number." When others call upon you, know that God's Grace is their sufficiency. The Grace of God that sent the call to you will meet that call; you yourself cannot heal a headache, but the Grace of God will perform the work that is given you to do. So when a call comes to you for a healing or a teaching, realize immediately that you alone do not know enough, but that the Grace of God will give you the answer. So do not hesitate to say, "Yes, I will give you help."

You will never fail to heal or teach or lead anyone to Truth if you continuously acknowledge *without false modesty* that it is the Grace of God that answers the call and that whatever spiritual grace you have is the Grace of God. Then the activity of God will make *Itself* evident, and the results will follow.

However, if you make the mistake of thinking you know enough to begin to teach, you will find that you will make a shipwreck of your experience, because you will never have enough understanding to heal or to teach. In fact, you never will be good enough! You cannot become that good! Not even Jesus was that good. He said, "Why callest thou me good?

There is but one good, the Father in Heaven. Why callest thou me spiritual? There is but one Spirit, the Father within. Why callest thou me a practitioner or a teacher or a master? There is but one Master, one Teacher, the Father within."

Now you can see why, even though you knew Truth, many times you may have tried to heal and not succeeded. It was because at that time you had only an intellectual knowledge of Truth. An intellectual knowledge of Truth will not work, because it is only a stepping-stone, only one of the means by which we achieve the spiritual realization of Truth.

Recently I was asked about founding a university to develop Infinite Way practitioners and teachers. I smiled and said, "I will consider it only if you are willing to make the course five to seven years and insist that the students live there seven days a week without vacations for five years, give me twenty-four hours a day of their lives, and do not go home or have any obligations of any kind." Why? Because I have found that if I have students three to five years, even six years, and if I have them enough days a week and enough hours in the day, they finally develop spiritual vision. I have never yet succeeded with any student in less time than that. True, some students became practitioners in twenty-four hours, but that was not through me. It was through their own inner development. The minute they turned to God, their souls opened and they evolved and began healing at once. But that was not because of my teaching; it had nothing to do with me! It was their own development. The same happened in Christian Science, long before The Infinite Way. Some Christian Scientists became very good practitioners after only six to nine months of work. But it was because of their own readiness and development; it was not because of the teacher.

Lacking such readiness and self-development, an individual must devote many years to attaining God-experience before he or she can be transformed into a perfect worker in the ministry and a capable practitioner. A desire only to teach or heal defeats the purpose. The desire must be only to attain the God-experience.

My inner unfoldment has revealed to me that the secret of life is attaining that mind that was in Christ Jesus, or at least some measure of it. It is the attaining of God-realization, the God-experience, the conscious communion with God, the ability to live and move and have your being in God, the ability to throw your entire dependence on the Infinite Invisible instead of on any person or circumstance in the outer.

So when a person comes to me with this object and without any thought of using it for public ministry or becoming a practitioner, I can work with and lead that student step by step to that experience. After that, the student can go out into the ministry if he or she wants to; or, as some have done, retire "back to the country" and never be seen by others, communing with God and doing work on the inner plane.

The Invisible Strength

Many of the miracles you are witnessing in the world today, and will witness in the future, are the direct result of mystics' conscious communion with God. They bring God into the visible world, appearing as modern wonders, although some of these are badly misused. Eventually, even the desire to misuse these wonders will disappear. You will witness peace on earth and see atomic power used for peaceful purposes and less for world-threatening bombs. You will see more willingness to conciliate, which is a sign not of weakness but of spiritual strength. When you are willing to forego the weapons of the world, it is because you have a greater dependence on the invisible weapon: the word of God, the sword of the Spirit. That is spiritual strength.

In the same proportion that you rely more on the Infinite Invisible, you will show forth greater health and harmony, with less reliance on medications and surgery. No one can say to you, "You must not use medicines, or you must not have surgery," because no one can make your demonstration for you. That is your individual experience. But in proportion as you receive spiritual light, you will depend less on medicines, less on personal advertising, less on physical and mental activities. You will relax more and more in an invisible spiritual presence and power.

As you attain more and more of spiritual light, you will depend less and less on legal processes. You will not go to court as much as you formerly did. As you attain more spiritual light, eventually you will be able to get along without courts, because whatever legal problems come to you will be solved. Of course, you may go to court to have something legalized or made official, but you will not go to court to fight for your rights or for what is coming to you. You will find that it will be offered you free willing, free grace, without fighting. As the God-experience comes into your life, spiritual power accompanies it and governs your whole experience.

Do not be discouraged because you have studied all those years in an effort to attain an intellectual knowledge of Truth. The paths you have followed may not have been the way to even an intellectual knowledge of Truth, because there are lots of errors in the various teachings. For example, it was once believed that you could demonstrate supply. The movement that taught so has shrunk almost to nonexistence in England and in this country, because no one ever succeeded in demonstrating supply. But by demonstrating a realization of God, you can have all the supply you will ever want. In the same way, you cannot demonstrate companionship or anything else.

You would be amazed at how many letters I receive saying, "Please do some work for me for health [or wealth or a husband]. Enclosed please find $2.00 [or $3.00 or $5.00]." I write to them, "I'm sorry, but I don't know how to get you health, wealth, or a husband for $5.00!" I do not know how to do it

even for $50.00! So I return their money, but I do write a para-
graph to this effect: "If, however, you feel that you would like to
know God, to experience God, write to me again, and I will
be happy to help you. When you do experience God, you will
probably find that you have your health, your wealth, or your
marriage."

You cannot reply to such letters, "Oh, yes! I'll take up work
for you to get a husband." If you succeed, just think how you
will be blamed when the husband does not turn out right! Or
you may demonstrate money for a person, and some parent
will write you, "Why did you do that? He got in trouble with
it!" So do not try to demonstrate money, health, or husband, or
some other thing. When you demonstrate the grace of God
for a person, then the money, the marriage, the position, or
whatever, that comes will be the result of spiritual unfoldment,
and it will be harmonious, joyous, and progressively good.

In The Infinite Way, let us demonstrate the realization of
God and forget about demonstrating anything else. You know,
there is no literature at the present time on how or when Jesus
achieved His spiritual realization, but we do know the story of
Saul of Tarsus. We do not know how John (of the Gospel of
John) attained his spiritual light. All we know is that he received
it directly from Jesus Christ. It is not likely that he received it
while Jesus was on earth. He received it in inner illumination,
and the minute he received it, he was able to write a book
about it. We have no record that he wrote books before that
time.

So it is. Attain some measure of that mind that was in
Christ Jesus, attain a God-experience, attain the ability to consciously commune inside with God. Talk to no man about it,
but find a teacher with whom you can speak or write, one who
can guide you. More especially, find one who has attained some
ability to meditate fruitfully, then meditate with that person.
You do not need instruction in the letter of Truth; you can find
all of that in the Bible and certainly in my The Infinite Way

writings. But if you can find someone who has attained the ability to touch the inner kingdom in their meditation, that person can open his or her spiritual center so that you too will be able to read with spiritual consciousness instead of only with the intellectual mind. You will then read with the heart or soul instead of only with the brain.

That is why in our work, we give most of our time and attention to meditation work. Whenever or wherever we have someone who has attained the ability to meditate and bring forth spiritual fruitage and harmony, we encourage that one to meditate with the students to help them open their souls, their consciousness, so that they in turn may be able to not only read books in spiritual consciousness but also eventually to write them.

We know how God-realization came to Saul of Tarsus. He had spent many years studying, reading, and praying about God. It would seem to us that he was doing it wrong because he was doing it in the Hebrew way. There was nothing wrong about that; he was doing it in a perfectly right way. The proof is that in one blinding flash, the full Light was given to him. That would not have happened if he had been doing everything wrong all those years. He was not! The Hebrew way, the Protestant way, the Catholic way, the Hindu way, the Mohammedan way—any way is all right *if* the desire is to know God. Certainly that was Saul's desire!

When we ourselves are willing to sacrifice our lives, our money, our time, and our effort, we too will someday lose any erroneous concept of God and find the one true God. That is what happened to Saul. In that blinding flash, he lost the Hebrew concept of God and gained the vision of the true God, the experience of God that is better than any concept of God. A concept can only be a concept; it can never be God! The best that any teaching can do for us is to lead us to the place where we realize that none of the concepts are correct. The only correct thing is the experience of God *Itself*. Then you will know how foolish it was to believe that your concept was correct.

When you have risen above the letter of Truth into the spirit of consciousness of Truth—that is, when you (like Saul) have left behind your studies of God and come into the experience of God—you will probably have an entirely different concept of God and you will be using different terms. In the early stages of many people's experience, God is thought of as spirit or soul. As you know, the revelation of God came to me as the Infinite Invisible.

In the same way, those who have learned all that the Truth books teach of God, prayer, and spirit and then have a God-experience, all they have read is wiped away and they begin to use their own terminology. They begin to write books showing how it came through to them. It may be the last word for them, but it is not the last word, because someone else will begin to write books showing it forth as the experience appeared to them. Walt Whitman did, Brother Lawrence did, Emerson did, Blake did, Francis Thompson did. Those who have had a God-experience suddenly begin to write books or poems. *The Oxford Book of English Mystical Verse*, Oxford Press, contains maybe a hundred authors who attained spiritual experience and began writing poetry.

Knowing the Truth and intellectually agreeing with it will not do the work for you. But by abiding in it, eventually you will pass from the letter of Truth to the actual experience or demonstration of spiritual discernment. In your many years of study, you may have been only agreeing intellectually with the Truth you have read, but have said, "I cannot prove these things; I cannot show them forth; I cannot even feel them!" That's alright! Everyone has gone through that phase, not for just a year or two or three; some have gone through it as much as seven or eight years, and it would not be surprising to find some who have gone through it for thirty years. You may ask,

"Is that what I have to look forward to?" Yes, there is that possibility, but why stop? You will have nothing to go back to, so you may as well stay on the path until it breaks, because if you stay with the correct letter of Truth, you will attain the spiritual wisdom you are seeking.

Christ as the Consciousness of Mankind

In the past we have thought of the coming of the Christ to individual consciousness as a rare experience. But the revelation has been given to me that we are at the beginning of a new era, which we will call "the second coming of the Christ"— the coming of the Christ to earth as the consciousness of all mankind.

Today, the Christ is being established as the universal consciousness, and we are witnessing on earth something that never before existed. Now it is less possible than ever before for people to do evil. Even as they only *think* of doing evil, the repercussion is upon them. In other words, there is already enough Christ established as human consciousness that the mere thought of doing evil is enough to bring a repercussion on the thinker.

In the three-dimensional life into which we were born, people could do all kinds of evil and experience very little punishment. That is why for so many generations there have been wars, slavery, and man's inhumanity to man. There has never been a righteous war. Every war ever fought has been an evil one, and the perpetrators did not suffer, only the victims did. However, now there is enough of the Christ functioning in human consciousness to wreak immediate vengeance upon those who perpetrate wrong. It is not the Christ wreaking vengeance on the perpetrators of evil; it is the perpetrators who are bringing upon themselves the penalty of their thoughts, motives, and deeds.

You cannot do a wrong unto the Christ without it immediately having its repercussions upon you, because evil is destroyed when it comes into the presence of the Christ. Remember that Judas Iscariot committed suicide within a very few days of his betrayal of the Master Jesus. Evil destroys those who cling to it. If we hold within ourselves some wrong intent, some wrong desire, some evil motive and think to profit from such evil, instead of seeking to be freed from it, heaven help us if we ever come up against anyone of spiritual light!

That is what is taking place in the world today, and from now on there will be fewer wars, less of man's inhumanity to man, less cheating, less stealing, less of robbing people of their birthright. There is so much spiritual loosed in human consciousness that those who have in mind the destruction of others, the holding of others in bondage to anything, are finding their punishment long before their plans succeed. That is happening throughout the world. The evildoers are coming up against someone of spiritual light; and when they do, they had better get ready for their funeral, because the Christ of your consciousness will do to them what it did unto Judas Iscariot! If a Judas will not let loose of his evil, he will be carried off with his evil. In all parts of the world there are those who still believe that it is perfectly alright to live by the sword. They are going to come up against the Christ and die by the sword, because the weapon they use against humanity is the very weapon that will cut them down. Those who are determined to cling to their evil and think to benefit from it will be destroyed along with the evil, because evil destroys those who cling to it.

However, those who relinquish the evil are healed. In our travels around the world, we come in contact with tens of thousands of people desirous of losing their sins, their diseases, their false appetites, their resentments, their jealousies, their envy, their malice, their lust, or their greed—and they are being healed. When we in sin come before those of spiritual light, sincerely wanting to be freed from such evil, we are healed rather than destroyed. If there is within our consciousness any evil, any wrong, and we are at the point where we would really like to be free of it, we need only seek someone who has attained some measure of spiritual light, and we will be forgiven our sin and be set free. Remember, however, that the Master said also, "Go and sin no more lest a worse thing come upon you."

Every bit of spiritual light that you individually attain increases the amount of Christ-consciousness that is loosed in the world. This is how it operates. I, if I be lifted up, draw all men unto me. If I have attained some measure of Christ-consciousness, those of you who are receptive and responsive may leave here with an uplift. It may be a physical, mental, moral, or some other kind of healing; or you may be lifted into a higher measure of Christ-consciousness—all by virtue of one individual being lifted up. Any measure of Light in my consciousness produces a spark of Light in the consciousness of those of you who are at all spiritually inclined.

When I have a group of students who have studied for years and have attained some measure of spiritual Light, this spiritual Light is reaching hundreds, and they are being drawn to the Light. When we have hundreds, then thousands are being drawn to the Light. You are a part of that pioneer movement.

Had it been said two thousand years ago that there would be ten to fourteen thousand people doing spiritual work on earth, I am sure that it would have been ridiculed. It was believed that only those whom God had visited could do so. Now we know that God is no respecter of persons. We have learned that it is possible for almost anyone to attain some measure of the Spirit of God. We have seen that the saints, the sages, the seers, the mystics are not the only ones who receive this Spirit. God visits anybody and everybody who can open their consciousness to receive that Presence which is within. That is why so many businesspeople, housewives, and others are spiritual healers and spiritual teachers.

You do not have to belong to any religion or church. You can, of course, belong to a church if you would like to do so, but belonging or not belonging to a church or religion has nothing to do with your relationship with God. Your relationship with God has to do with an activity of your own consciousness in which you realize, "I and the Father are one," which is a universal truth. We are all of the household of God, and God is available to us in the degree that we open ourselves to His Presence.

In Christian Science, in Unity, in New Thought, and in The Infinite Way, we have been proving for the past hundred years that one individual imbued with Truth can bring healing of mind, body, pocketbook, or human relations to thousands of patients or students.

I remember sitting in meditation with one practitioner and, within three months, being healed of a disease that was supposed to have killed me within three months. I can remember sitting in meditation with another practitioner and being so completely lifted out of my old selfhood that I never again could smoke, drink, gamble, or do any of the ordinary things that were a part of my businessman's life. It was an experience that led me right into this spiritual work. Think now for a moment of the influence these practitioners had on one life (mine), and then think of all the patients or students with whom they worked over a period of years!

What sets these practitioners apart from the rest of mankind? What sets apart the practitioners, the teachers, or any of the metaphysical or spiritual writers you have known? What sets them so apart that they could bring about the healing of the body, the mind, the character, the morals, or the pocketbook? It was their transition from "man whose breath is in his nostrils" to "that mind which has its being in Christ." In some way and for some reason, they were first drawn to the study of Truth through books, lectures, classes, and teachings. Eventually, something happened within them that they probably could not describe. But at some particular moment in their experience, they attained a degree of spiritual consciousness, or Christ-consciousness. They attained some measure of the transcendental (that which is beyond the human).

Those of you who have been with me many years know that I experienced this "transition" while in the presence of a man who, having received such spiritual Light, was a very great and famous healer. He never seemed to understand what had taken place within him, but he could let it take place and produce healing work. But not understanding it, he never undertook teaching work.

For the past thirty-some years, I have seen many in Christian Science and in Unity who had the desire to heal, to teach, and to give to others, but they could not. Now I am witnessing them in the Infinite Way. I say to them, "Be patient! You will be able to, but you must wait until the Spirit of the Lord God is upon you and you are ordained to do these things." When the Master parted from His disciples, He said to them, "Remain in this city until you are imbued from on high, until the Spirit of the Lord God is upon you."

We cannot function as practitioners or spiritual teachers until we have received spiritual illumination—the actual experience of the Christ, of the transcendental Presence. If we lack that one essential, even though we have the will, the desire, and the hope, we cannot heal, reform, or enrich. Until that experience which sets us apart takes place within our consciousness, we must be perfectly content to remain students. When you actually have the experience of the Christ, the transcendental Presence, you will be successful as a practitioner, healer, teacher, and so on in the measure of your fidelity to the Christ, the transcendental Presence.

You will know when the Spirit is consciously upon you by the fruitage in your experience and when those who come within range of your consciousness detect that you have something they lack. At first, someone in your family or among your friends or neighbors will begin to ask what it is you have, or ask you to share it with them, or even ask you for help.

Any measure of spiritual Light that is raised up in you immediately begins to raise up some member of your family, a neighbor, a friend, a relative, or a stranger. If you have been lifted up by so much as one grain, then as you go forth, you are carrying that grain of spiritual Light out into the world. And any degree of sin, disease, lack, limitation that touches your consciousness immediately begins to dissolve, and others get healings. All this bears witness to the fact that the measure of Christ raised up in an individual is the measure of Christ loosed in the consciousness of others that raises them up.

The Kingdom of God Established on Earth

We are now in an age in which there is a greater measure of Christ in the world, and children are being born into this world. In another generation there will be so much Christ in the human consciousness that you will witness it. You will witness the Kingdom of God established on earth. There will be no more darkness, no more sin, no more disease. There will be no more death, only a transition from the visible into the invisible. We remain in the visible as long as we have a mission to perform in the visible. And when that mission is accomplished, we pass from the visible into the invisible. We continue to live, but on a higher spiral of spiritual life.

Eternal Life

Let me illustrate this so that you will no longer merely believe in immortality, you will actually experience it. Visualize, if you will, a tree—any kind of tree. On that tree are seeds, and the life of the tree is the life of the seed. When the seed is carried somewhere and falls to the earth and sinks to the ground, it becomes a tree. The life of this second tree is not a different life. It is the same life that was of the first tree as well as the life of its seed. Go back over this in your mind until it is very clear to you that the life of the first tree is the same life as that of its seeds. Therefore, it is the same life of tree number two, and it is the same life of its seed, which in turn is the same life of tree number three. We have three trees, but there is only one life. When you look at a tree, you cannot see the life; you can see only the body of the tree.

Your Selfhood

Your selfhood is your invisible force or being. You cannot see this self when you look in a mirror. What you see in the mirror is merely a body: it is not you. You are what is described in the word *I*. "I" is what constitutes you. It is the life of your body. It is what gives your body its direction. When your body drops away, the "I" of you does not drop off, for the "I" is your life force, your being. The "I" immediately takes on a new body. As you step forth from your present body, you may find yourself in a body that is a bit strange to you because the "I," being incorporeal, spiritual life, is of no particular sex. Only the body is male or female. Then, too, your new body will be suitable to the atmosphere in which you will now function. If you are then functioning on earth, your body will probably be similar to your present one. But if you are then functioning in a different environment, your body will be strange to you. However, you will recognize that I am "I." You will realize that you are you, and you will get used to having a different body in which and through which to function.

The more you realize that the life of a tree is immortal—that its life is the very life of the seed and the life of the next tree—the more you will realize your own immortality, and you will immediately recognize that the life of your child and of your grandchild is immortal. Even before your child is born—and long before your grandchild is born—you will be carrying in consciousness the truth of the immortal and spiritual nature of the life of this unborn child, and this child will be born into immortality. Do you not see that "ye shall know the truth and the truth shall set you free"? But only as you *know* the truth shall it set you free: Know thy self to be spirit, to be immortal life. Then you will understand the message that Christ Jesus gave to this world: "I am come that you might have life and that you might have life more abundantly." "I" am come. That "I" in the midst of you is the He that is come to bring you more abundant life—that is, life eternal. The "I" is life eternal, whether it is in the visible or in the invisible.

Now, if "I" am immortal, eternal, spiritual life, then that life of me is the Christ-life, or the presence of the Christ. And since Christ is your identity and since God is my Father and yours, Christ is universal identity. By recognizing the Christ of your being, you now have Christ on earth instead of mortal man. In the moment that you acknowledge this, you loose more of the Christ into human consciousness and you are establishing the reign of Christ on earth.

Ever since this was revealed to me within, I have known that we are witnessing the second coming of the Christ to universal human consciousness. Christ is now coming to earth as the consciousness of *all* mankind, not only to the consciousness of saints and sages and to the few who become practitioners and teachers. If ten righteous persons (that is, ten spiritually illumined persons) can save a city, imagine what four hundred can do by going out into the world acknowledging, "Christ liveth my life, and those who touch my life, touch Christ. By virtue of 'I and the Father being one,' those who touch my life and come within the orbit of my consciousness, are lifted up spiritually." By acknowledging this for yourself, you bring the harmonies that automatically follow the reign of Christ not only to yourself but also to the entire world.

So you see, in order to save the world, it is not necessary to try to reach mankind. It is only necessary to raise up the Christ in our selves and realize Christ in each other. The first step leading toward this is to fill your consciousness with Truth.

We can have no one speak the word of Truth who cannot demonstrate it. First must come the actual experience of God and then healing work before a student can undertake teaching work. Practitioners or teachers of The Infinite Way must, by their presence, bring healing—physical, mental, moral, financial. They must do this, otherwise they have not been endowed by the Spirit. By their healing ability, we know that the Spirit has touched them and has given them the ability to present this message of The Infinite Way.

When the message of The Infinite Way was given to me, I was also given instructions for carrying it to the world. The first instruction was, "Never seek a student. Share with the students who come to you, but never seek a student." Not only do I never attempt to seek a student, but also in all of these years I have never gone anyplace to lecture or teach except when I was sent for and when the invitation indicated seriousness of purpose.

This is the way it worked out. I did not move out of my small office in California. First, three people walked in the door and asked for instruction. Later, four couples came and asked for instruction. I continued to wait in my office until the next came seeking instruction, and the next, and the next. In all of these years, I discovered that all that is necessary for the unfoldment of the message of The Infinite Way (or even for whatever there is of my personal life) is done without my taking conscious thought, without my planning. When I attain in my meditation the realization of the Presence of God, the Spirit of God, or my oneness or union with God, in that moment I am set free from all human efforts.

Only as our students show forth by their lives that they are ready for such an experience can they come to it. So I say to our students, "Study, practice, meditate. Do not try to be workers in the world field until you are endowed from on high. Do not go out to preach, to proselyte. Do nothing!" Why?

There is undoubtedly a great danger to those on the spiritual path. Some receive a touch of the Spirit, and before they have had an opportunity to assimilate it, to grow in Grace, they run around the world trying to do good with it. This should not be! Be patient! Grow in Grace! Remain in this city until you know that the Spirit of God is working through you. The proof, the indication, of this is the measure of service for which you are called upon.

There are some who, when the Spirit first touches them, believe that they have become righteous or spiritual or moral or good or benevolent and are tempted to glorify their own egos. Some have gone out into the world and built a personal following. That has no relationship to spiritual work! Some allow their ego to misinterpret the realization of God's Grace and have lost their hope of heaven.

CHAPTER 3

THE CHRIST MINISTRY

It is sometimes questioned whether or not God means for us to enjoy the good things of life such as harmony, peace, health, safety, and protection. There are hundreds of theological books written on the subject of "God's will for man." Not one book written by men in the theological world states one iota of truth on the subject of the will of God. These men have not accepted the Truth given us by Jesus Christ, and only Jesus Christ has revealed the truth.

He said, "I have come to do the will of my Father." What is the will of the Father? Jesus said unto His disciples:

Go and shew John again those things which ye do hear and see:

The blind receive their sight, and the lame walk, the lepers are cleansed, and the deaf hear, and the dead are raised up, and the poor have the gospel preached to them. (Matthew 11:5)

That is the will of God for man! Never let anyone tell you that God's will for man is not good! Never let anyone tell you that it is God's will that you be punished for any sin that you have committed. The Master's ministry was one of healing and forgiveness. He forgave the woman taken in adultery and the thief on the cross. He taught the message of forgiving seventy-times-seven, praying for those who despitefully use you, praying for those who persecute you, praying for those who wrong you, praying for your enemies. That was the Christ's ministry, and that is the will of the Father.

It is just as right for us to enjoy health, harmony, security, and supply now as it was right for those who received these blessings through "that mind which was also in Christ Jesus." That same Spirit that animated the disciples and enabled them to heal later enabled Paul to heal, reform, save, lift up, and even send supply to seven churches.

That same Spirit that raised Jesus Christ from the dead—the God of Abraham, of Isaac, and of Jacob—is available here and now, in this day and age, just as it was two thousand years ago and has always been throughout all time, even though it has been ignored by man. That same Spirit exists in this room, in your home, in your church, or wherever you may be, because It exists within you and you carry it with you wherever you travel. It is closer to you than breathing, nearer than hands and feet, and It is available now, as It always has been, to bring to you that "peace which passeth all understanding"—that Peace that actually reveals to us health, harmony, wholeness, completeness, perfection, and joy and quickens our mortal body.

The world is full of the Presence of God, yet there are people sinning, suffering, and dying and this Presence and Power of God does nothing for them. It never will unless that same Spirit that was in Jesus, John, Peter, and the others is brought to light in and through the activity of the consciousness of an individual. Many have believed that the Presence of God is available, many have trusted in the Presence and Power of God, but few individuals are capable of bringing that Spirit into conscious expression in our experience and to our bodies, to our minds. Remember that there must be a *now*, as there was a *then*, an individual who, like Peter, John, Jesus, Abraham, Isaac, or Jacob, can bring that same Spirit into activity in our experience. That is the journey upon which we have embarked.

Attaining Inner Realization

Those of you who have witnessed or experienced spiritual healing realize that it was brought about by the realization of the Spirit of an individual whom we may call practitioner, teacher, leader, or minister. The healing, the performing, the saving processes do not take place until that Spirit is brought to light in and through the consciousness of an individual. Remember that!

We must therefore attain some measure of that mind, that Spirit, that was in Christ Jesus until *It* acts through us to raise up those who are crippled, deaf, poor, or in sin. As students of The Infinite Way, it is our function to study, pray, and meditate until we attain some measure of that Christhood and, through that Spirit, bring about the healing or reforming or saving that rightfully belongs to those who come to us for help.

We do not try to help everyone for whom someone else requests help, because in order to benefit, the individual must first open his or her consciousness to receive the Christ. Just as there must be an individual spiritually endowed to bring help, so must the individual who seeks help open his or her consciousness to receive the Spirit. You would not want someone to intrude into your consciousness and try to make you accept some medical remedy that he *knows* would cure you if only you would take it! Everyone must be allowed the privilege of opening or not opening their consciousness to the Christ.

Remember that the Master said, "I stand at the door and knock." The individual must open his consciousness to the

Christ and admit us. So as a general rule, adopt this principle: When someone requests help for an aunt, uncle, nephew, niece, child, or friend, be sure to reply, "Certainly I will, as long as *they* request it, but I will not intrude upon their consciousness."

There are thousands of men and women on earth today who have attained some measure of this Christ-Spirit and are healing the sick, reforming the sinner, bringing an increased sense of supply to those who lack. The measure of their ability is, of course, dependent upon the degree of their awareness, the degree of their dedication to the Christ principle. We do not know of anyone who is bringing forth the same degree of healing as did the Master, so it is questionable whether there is anyone on earth at the present time who has attained the full measure of the Christ-Spirit.

The Master, Christ Jesus, attained God-realization in its fullness. It is because He attained that Spirit in its fullness that His healing and supplying work, His feeding of the hungry, His healing of the sick were of such magnitude. His disciples did not achieve the same fullness of Christhood as did the Master, and so their healings never approached the same level.

The Infinite Way's teaching is that it is possible today for each one of us to develop some measure of Christ-realization. Some will attain it to a great degree; some, to a lesser degree. But it is possible for any man, any woman, and, more especially, any child to become consciously aware of God, to feel within themselves that the same Spirit that was in Christ-realization will be attained in proportion to the number of quiet periods during the day or night that they turn within themselves and invite the Father to reveal Himself to them. It may take days, weeks, months to finally achieve such inner realization or unfoldment, but I can tell you that it is worth waiting for, striving for, and struggling for. "The way is narrow and few there be that enter it," but with patience, devotion, and wanting God-realization, we can be one of those few. In The Infinite

Way, we do not seek the demonstration of things or conditions. We seek the demonstration of God *Itself*, because when we have God, we have all things. In The Infinite Way, under no circumstances do we appeal to God for help or material things, nor do we use mental or spiritual powers to obtain these things. Our only objective is to attain some measure of the Spirit that was in Christ Jesus.

At first, it may be difficult to discern the message of The Infinite Way, because The Infinite Way reverses most of what we have been taught, first in orthodox religious teachings and then in metaphysical teachings. Even the language we use may confuse you, so first we have to throw out of our minds all the meanings we have formerly attributed to these terms and try to understand what we of The Infinite Way mean when we use these words. For example, when we use the word *God*, we do not mean what the world understands to be God. We use the word in the same way, and we spell it in the same way, but we do not mean what orthodox teachings or metaphysical teachings mean. We also use the word *prayer*, but when you understand what we mean by prayer, you will hardly recognize it, because it has no relationship at all to what the dictionary says prayer is or what the church says prayer is. *God, Christ, prayer, meditation, communion*—we use all these words but in a different sense, and this makes it difficult to perceive the message of The Infinite Way. Therefore, we have to make a transition in consciousness, and this takes time and effort.

> *Neither do men put new wine into old bottles; else the bottles break, and the wine runneth out, and the bottles perish: but they put new wine into new bottles, and both are preserved.* (Matthew 9:17)

You must be willing to clean out the "old bottles" of your consciousness, because you cannot acquire a new consciousness if you try to mix the old with the new.

Prayer as Taught by the Master

The Master, Christ Jesus, taught us that we are not to ask God for anything but spiritual bread—that is, spiritual understanding or spiritual realization. He taught that we are not to pray for our friends but for our enemies, because it avails you nothing to pray for your friends. He taught that we must not pray until we have established peace with our fellowman. In other words, when you acknowledge that you love your neighbor as yourself, you are asking God's Grace not only for yourself, not only for your friends, but for all those who are reaching toward spiritual realization, whether they be friends or enemies.

Christ's ministry was one of forgiveness. He condemned no man. It is not God's will that people be punished for their sins, but that they be forgiven.

> Neither do I condemn thee: go, and sin no more. (John 8:11)
> He that is without sin among you, let him cast the first stone. (John 8:7)
> Man, who made me judge over thee? (Luke 12:14)

The Master taught us to forgive, forgive, forgive—seventy-times-seven—to pray for our enemies that they be forgiven, not punished; to pray for those who despitefully use us and persecute us; to pray for our enemies—personal, national, racial, or religious. Never are we permitted to wish them evil or even believe that they deserve punishment for their sins.

We are told that when we go to the altar of prayer, if we remember that any man has aught against us, we are to get up and leave. First, we must make peace with our fellowman and then return to the altar. As long as we entertain hate, enmity, jealousy, revenge, and such feelings, we are not at peace with others. In order to pray to our Heavenly Father, the Father within us, it is necessary that we come with clean hands.

Before the Christian missionaries came to Hawaii, the Hawaiians had only spiritual healing. Each group within a community had a priest who would call them together twice a year. He would line them up in front of him and ask each one, "Have you had any trouble with anyone in this group in the past six months?" If the answer was, "Yes," he would instruct, "Make peace now. Begin forgiving him or asking for his forgiveness!" And then, "Have you entertained any jealousy or animosity? Begin now by asking forgiveness and by forgiving!" And, "Have you had lust or animality toward anyone? Start now asking forgiveness and by forgiving!" Thus, each person was compelled to purge himself and herself of these negative human emotions. They were then told, "Now the peace of God can begin to flow in your minds and bodies. Without this, you are blocking entrance to the Divine Grace." Is it not this that the Master taught us?

You will find that when you come to the throne pure in spirit, God's Grace flows freely in your consciousness, in your mind, in your soul, in your spirit, and then it can raise your body. You have purged yourself of human fear, human hate, human desire, human jealousy, human animosity. You have declared that the Spirit of God dwells in you, that you love your fellowman, your neighbor, even as you love yourself, and do not hold him or her in condemnation or as deserving punishment for sins but rather that these sins be forgiven because, "Father, they know not what they do."

The Infinite Way Concept of Prayer

Having prayed for spiritual realization, having prayed that our enemies be forgiven, having established peace with our fellowman and loving our neighbor as ourselves, having forgiven those who abuse us, we are ready to open that inner ear so that we may hear the still, small Voice. That is The Infinite Way concept of prayer: Prayer is not the words we speak, but the still, small Voice of God uttering *It*self to us.

The Voice does not always utter words or sounds. Sometimes we are not even aware of *It* until we see the wonderful effect *It* produces. Sometimes *It* does speak in words; other times *It* just gives us an inner peace that assures us that God is on the field.

It makes no difference how we receive *It*. An assurance always comes that God is with us—Emmanuel, God with us. Then we remember, "*I* will never leave you nor forsake you. *I* will be with you until the end of the world." As we remember those assurances, the Voice speaks within us, or we feel that Divine something, that Divine assurance within. Then we see peace where there was war, discord, or inharmony. We see prosperity where there was lack. But we have not prayed *for* these things.

First we have purified ourselves, then the real prayer begins. The highest sense of prayer is *listening,* not speaking or thinking, but listening. Nothing happens until He utters His Voice within us, then comes what we call demonstration. It is a demonstration of God's Presence, although it appears as health, harmony, wholeness, completeness, perfection, or some other form of good.

When this inner Grace takes over and goes before us to make the crooked places straight and does all things for us, then we have entered a period of life called living by Grace.

In The Infinite Way, our goal is to attain the spiritual consciousness that enables us to live by Grace. How do we attain that state of consciousness that enables us to receive this Divine Grace? How do we receive the Presence and Power of God within us? How do we attain the consciousness that brings God into our individual experience? We cannot achieve it vicariously. No minister, priest, rabbi, teacher, or practitioner can do the work for us. Listening to a lecture or a teacher or minister will not do it. They can only help us along the way.

We attain this goal by individually preparing ourselves by conscious remembrance, keeping the mind stayed on God, acknowledging God in all ways, meditating, purifying ourselves of human tendencies, opening ourselves constantly so that the Voice of God can utter *Itself* within us. Then we shall live by the Grace of an inner Presence and an inner Power that does all things for us. "He performeth that which is given me to do. He perfecteth that which concerneth me." So, we must listen and put into practice what we have learned until we attain "that mind which was also in Christ Jesus," until we attain the consciousness of the Presence of God.

CHAPTER 4

MEDITATION: THE KEY TO
THE MINISTRY WITHIN

When you look around, as I did, and see millions of people praying and attending church and yet see so much sin, disease, and death on earth, you know that no external form of worship can be the way. External forms of prayer have not brought sinlessness, peace, harmony, or brotherly love on earth at any time in recorded history. There have been intervals without war here and there, but perhaps at no one time has there been an absence of war everyplace.

When you see this state of the world, one of two things must happen to you. You either lose all hope for man on earth, for the balm of Gilead, and say let us eat, drink, and be merry for tomorrow we die. Or you must come to the realization that there must be another way and that you must discover it. That is the realization I came to.

For many years I did not know how to bring God into individual experience—how to bring the comfort and the healing that the Master promised, the raising of the dead that the Master promised, the forgiveness of sin that the Master promised, the life eternal that the Master promised. These were only words in a book!

Then there came to me the experience that brought with it the actual realization that the presence of God was within, with many signs following. Of course, this was only a first step leading to the final realization that whatever of God you experience must be experienced within your own consciousness. You will not find God in a holy mountain or a holy city or a holy temple or a holy book or a holy teacher. You will find the Kingdom of God within yourself, or you will not find it in this lifetime!

Scripture refers to an inspired state of consciousness as a mountaintop. When Moses received his great revelation of God, he did not receive it in a place. He found it within his own consciousness, not out in the air and not in any holy temple. He was just on a mountaintop. It may have been a physical mountaintop, or it may have been a mental one. But certainly he discovered God—the realm of God, the activity of God, the presence of God—within himself. Later Isaiah was led to say, "Is there any God beside me? I know not any. The only God there is dwells *within* me." Paul later phrased it differently, "I can do all things through *Christ that dwelleth in me*," and, "I live, yet not I; *Christ that dwelleth in me* lives my life."

Wherever you find a spiritual leader or master or revelator who is not interested in glorifying himself or herself or building an institution to be worshipped, you will find the same revelation: "The Kingdom of God is within me," but not in the sense that the Kingdom of God is within this master only and not within you. The Kingdom of God that is within me is within you as well. We must find this Kingdom of God that is within our own consciousness—not in a consciousness of someone who was on earth two thousand years ago, or twenty-five hundred years ago, or four thousand years ago. Unless we find the Kingdom of God that is within our own consciousness, it cannot exist for us! No experience can take place in our lives except through our own consciousness. The Kingdom of God may exist for our neighbor and for those who followed Buddha or Jesus or Isaiah or John or Paul, but it cannot exist for us until we have searched for and found the Kingdom of God within our own consciousness. The Master was very explicit. The Kingdom of God is neither "lo, here!" nor "lo, there!" It has to be found within you.

This unfoldment that took place within me, because I did not find it in any book, revealed itself in just this way: As an individual I must expect sin, disease, lack, death, war, danger, accident, infection, and contagion—the same as everyone else in the world must expect it! If there is any way to be free from such conditions, it must be found through bringing God into my experience. How is that done?

Since I had already experienced the presence of God, it was only a matter of listening, being attentive, until more and more revelations came. This led to the discovery of meditation. I nearly said rediscovery of meditation, because meditation was known in the Orient for thousands of years, and at many times during those years meditation was a very fruitful practice. During the last century or two, the fruitfulness of meditation has nearly disappeared from the earth. But with the realization, at least in our experience, that meditation is the way, the fruitfulness of meditation has returned.

The science or art of active meditation is a fruitful experience with signs following. If there are no signs following, it means that meditation has not yet been attained, even though you have spent hours with your eyes closed. Closing the eyes and becoming still is not all there is to meditation. Meditation is a specific act that brings forth spiritual fruitage.*

---

*Editor's note: Serious students are referred to Joel S. Goldsmith's *The Art of Meditation* (New York: Harper & Row, 1956).

The Fruitage of God-Realization

If you view the world, as I have, as a world cut off from God and without a God to stop sin, disease, death, wars, accidents, and man's inhumanity to man, then you will be able to follow this experience individually and see how, ultimately, God-realization will be the salvation of man on earth. Eventually, it will restore complete peace to this earth. Those students who have been with us in many parts of the world have actually witnessed the love, the joy, the sharing, and the freedom that exist among students of The Infinite Way. They can testify that we individually, and to some extent collectively, are proving the fruitage of meditation, the fruitage of God-realization. Without the spiritual bond that is between us—that is, the realization of God's presence—the relationship that has existed for so many years among the students of The Infinite Way in all parts of the world could not have been maintained for so long. It is the Spirit of God that is the cement of our relationship. It is God-realization that has freed us from greed, hate, desire, lust, animality and from all possible injustice. This relationship is not brought about because we are a group of good people. Thinking this would be sacrilegious, because it would imply that we are better than others, and that is not true! Even the Master said, "Why callest thou me good?" and "I can of mine own self do nothing." So let us not rejoice in our own goodness.

There is only one good—the Father in heaven. We have no qualities of good of our own. Any quality of good that we have is God expressing Himself. We have no virtues of our own—no benevolence of our own, no intelligence of our own, no life of our own, no soul of our own, no purity of our own, no charity of our own. Whatever good there is in us is the Grace of God being expressed.

That is why in The Infinite Way we do not use titles to set ourselves above others. We are all students on the spiritual path—disciples, if we wish to call ourselves that, in varying degrees. The degree of Christhood attained is determined by one's devotion. There may be many students with far more understanding than some of our practitioners but who do not wish to become public practitioners or teachers.

We use such titles merely to indicate our function and to let it be known that we may be called upon by those who seek help. The title "practitioner" or "teacher" therefore does not indicate that we have more influence with God or are holier than thou. A title merely indicates that we are available day or night, Saturdays, Sundays, or holidays.

We our own selves can do nothing. We can only become the instruments through which the Spirit of God moves upon the face of the globe. We become instruments through which the Spirit of God reaches the ankles of the crippled man, the eyes of the blind, the ears of the deaf. We become the instruments through which God utters His Voice and the Spirit of God performs the healing and the redemption. We ourselves are not healers. No man or woman on earth can heal. Even Peter and John acknowledged this when they said:

> Ye men of Israel, why marvel ye at this? or why look ye so earnestly on us, as though by our own power or holiness we had made this man walk? (Acts 3:12)

The Father doeth the work. God is the healer! So in our work we say that we do not heal, but we can pray—the prayer of forgiveness, the prayer of releasing our enemies. Then we can listen until God utters His Voice within us. When the Voice within us speaks, the healing or the harmony or the peace takes place. We are merely the instruments through which God's Grace flows; we are not the healers. But let me assure you that only those who attain a consciousness of God's Presence, who attain the ability to be still and hear that Voice, can become instruments.

The spiritual life is sometimes called the "withinness"—the interior life, the inner life, the inner kingdom. The Master sometimes refers to it as "My Kingdom which is not of this world." My Kingdom is an inner kingdom. Remember that Christ indwells; therefore, the Christ Kingdom is within you. So if you want to receive forgiveness for your sins, do not look for forgiveness anywhere externally, but seek it from the Kingdom of God, the Christ Kingdom, which is within you. If you are seeking healing, even while you are accepting the help of the consciousness of one further advanced than yourself, remember to turn within.

Healing is an activity of the ministry of the Christ. "I am come to heal the sick, raise the dead, feed the hungry, forgive the sinner." This *I*, this Christ Kingdom, is within you. "I can do all things through the Christ which dwells in me, and the Christ ministry is within me." This means you! The Christ ministry—the Christ healing ministry, the Christ forgiving ministry, the Christ raising-of-the-dead ministry, the Christ feeding ministry—is within you. Therefore I give it to you as a principle on which the entire Infinite Way teaching is based. *You must turn to the Christ ministry for healing, for salvation, for forgiveness, for food, housing, and transportation, for healing of sin, disease, death.* You must turn to the Christ ministry, which is within yourself, for it.

Christ is not a man; Christ is the Spirit of God in you. You need take no thought for your life or for what you shall eat or drink or wherewithal you shall be clothed. You need only to turn within, and when you hear the words, "I will never leave thee nor forsake thee," or when you have the feeling of "My peace I give unto thee," your healing has been accomplished, your sins have been forgiven. The still, small Voice in one way or another utters, "Thy sins be forgiven thee." The Word of God, which is uttered through the Son of God within you, says, "Knowest not thou art the temple of the living God, thy body is the temple of the living God?"

Reading these words in a book or hearing them spoken may not always be the healing agency. They can be, if they have come forth from the consciousness of one in the Spirit. But remember that nothing can ever take the place of your receiving the Word within yourself. It is your permanent contact with the Kingdom of God. From the moment that this contact is made within you, you are no longer under the laws of weather, climate, age, food, or other physical laws—you are under Grace.

So meditation is not merely closing the eyes and stilling the mind. Meditation is that actual contact in consciousness that enables us to hear the still, small Voice that is within us and enables us to be fed by It. Just think! "The Christ is the bread, the meat, the wine, the water," and the Christ is within you. Therefore, to be spiritually fed, you must be fed from within. We are told that man must live by every Word of God. Now you know to what we must dedicate our lives. You are not dedicating your life to a person or to a book or a set of books. You are dedicating your life to attaining an inner stillness whereby the Word of God may utter Itself to you, in you, and through you to others.

Man shall not live by any human factor, nor by baubles, nor by the goodwill of other people. It was this revelation, with all of the signs following, that brought me to this message. I discovered that as a human being, I was cut off from God and knew all of the evils of humanhood. But as soon as I made this inner contact, something took over the living of my life, and I was spared about 90 percent of the evils of this world. Of course, some evils continued to come "nigh my dwelling place," but they were not of the major nature that most of this world suffers. I have problems now and then, yes. But remember that each problem that comes to us now is only another opportunity to go deeper into that Spirit and bring forth more of the Word. Without occasional problems, we would just rest on our laurels and begin to believe how good we are or how set apart we are. That is nonsense! We are in danger in any moment in which we glorify our own understanding or come to believe, "Now I have it!" Be assured that no one ever has it! You can live only one moment at a time; and every moment you have to decide whether you will live by the Spirit, by Grace, or whether you will come under the influence of the universal hypnotism or mesmerism that binds us to the pains or pleasures of the flesh. Every moment of our lives we are making this decision. Be assured that if we do not return over and over again during the day and the night to the center of our being for fresh inspiration, eventually we will find ourselves living on yesterday's manna, and then we are in danger. When we live on what we knew yesterday or the God contact that we had yesterday, we are in danger.

Why do you think the Master, even in His highly advanced spiritual stage, nevertheless went apart from His disciples, from the multitudes, for a weekend, perhaps for forty days? If Christ in His high mystical state of consciousness had to go apart to pray at noon and at night, you can understand why Paul admonishes us to "pray without ceasing." That means we must return again and again to the Kingdom of God that is within us for fresh manna.

I could never carry on my personal life, much less carry on this work, if I did not have many periods in the day and some in the night to return again and again to the center of my being for renewal, for refreshment, for Sabbath. What I knew yesterday is yesterday's manna. When I come to you, it must be with fresh manna from a God contact made five minutes ago, fifteen minutes ago, or while sitting in your presence. Only my latest God contact is the spiritual food that I may offer you, not the God contact I had yesterday or last week. I personally could not live twenty-four hours without constantly renewing myself at the source of my being. As I receive refreshment from the constant contact with the Christ within, I am enabled to not only live my life but also to share with those of you who are receptive and responsive.

Set this up as a definite Truth for yourself. The only thing you have to give to anyone is what you draw forth from the

Kingdom of God, the Christ ministry, with you. You cannot forgive sin, but the Christ ministry within you can if you make yourself a vehicle for it. You cannot heal the sick or raise the dead, but the Christ ministry functioning through you can. But you must continually make this contact. Pray without ceasing! Turn within!

The time will indeed come when you may need no words or thoughts to make and maintain this contact. You may need only to close your eyes and immediately get into the Spirit. But again, there are times when it is necessary to consciously remember that "my Kingdom is not of this world; the Christ Kingdom is of the world within me. I must get within in order that the Christ Kingdom may flow out through me; and I cannot live by bread alone, by externals, not by reading books or by even writing them! I must live by every Word that proceeds out of the mouth of God—the Word that I am receptive to today, this evening, now, in the middle of the night, and not the Word I received yesterday or the day before. I live and move and have my being by the Divine Inspiration that I receive from within me." That is the purpose of meditation. You cannot receive Divine Inspiration without meditation. You can try all you like to know God through your intellect or through knowledge and meditation. You will succeed only as you actually hear the Word within you. It may be a very long time before you hear it or feel it. But time is not of the essence.

Eternal Existence Is Ours

One of the greatest myths of religious teaching is that man lives three score and ten years. Of course, some do live three score and twenty and even three score and thirty. All of that is a myth. The life of individual you never began and will never end. What you are experiencing is one little parenthesis of your

life, and there will be many more of them. You lived before, and
you will live again. Life is the Eternal Being made manifest as
the individual you. There is no such thing as God setting a person on this earth and saying, "Now live for a few years until I
get ready to kill you!"

We do live in what we on this plane call life spans. We
call the stages of the life span: infancy, childhood, adulthood,
maturity, and advanced maturity. The truth is that we do not go
through these stages only once. We lived many life spans before
this one, and we will live many life spans after this one.
Therefore, what we are doing now is not laying up treasures to
last us just for the balance of our days on earth. We are laying
up a treasure of spiritual consciousness that will carry us
through infinite, eternal life. This treasure is the foundation of
eternal existence. We do not remember our previous existences
because we lived them wholly on the human plane. We had
not advanced on the spiritual plane and therefore carry no remembrance of previous life spans. But it will be different from
now on. You will carry your spiritual development of this life
into your next experience. Your spiritual development of this
lifetime will be the foundation for the greater spiritual awareness that will follow.

Never believe that men like Buddha, Christ Jesus, Isaiah,
John, or Paul came into this world and attained their spiritual
awareness sometime between the cradle and the grave. Nobody
could attain such a degree of spiritual illumination unless they
had laid the foundation for it in some previous existence. Their
spiritual illumination merely came to fruitage in their lifetimes;
they may have been perfecting it for several lifetimes.

Be assured that the spiritual foundation you are building
now, the spiritual treasures you are now laying up in your consciousness, is the basis of all that is to come. Do you believe
for a moment that whatever spiritual light I am receiving at
this time and for the last thirty years will all of a sudden be

snuffed out someday and no trace of it left? Can you believe for a moment that a person receives Divine Illumination and that it is later snuffed out? No!

All that has been given to me in these thirty years or more I will carry with me as a foundation for whatever experience is to come to me, whenever it comes. I am in no hurry to leave this plane, but I know the day will come when I will leave it. I also know that every bit of Light that has been given me is the Light that will go with me, and before me, and will be my spiritual treasure throughout all the ages to come. Because I have attained the ability to commune with my Father within me, I will carry with me throughout all time this ability to be consciously one with my Source, to be fed and clothed and housed spiritually. My body, whatever its form may be, will be a temple of God. This could never happen without this inner contact, this inner communion, with the Father, with the Christ ministry that is within me. The same ministry is within you.

Once you have attained the contemplative and communion state of meditation, do not believe for a moment that you will live on cloud nine continuously. There will be occasional drops to cloud one or cloud two, and I have known of occasions when one drops into the very depths of hell!

There is a need for this, or it would not happen. It happens so that the ego does not get too great. When the belief comes that one has become spiritual or holy, something has to happen to teach us that no one is ever holy or spiritual or "good." The very moment that the temptation comes to feel important, we have to be dropped right back so that humility comes to us and we remember that it is the Grace of God that is operating through us. We are only the transparency through which the Grace of God operates.

Make any and every sacrifice necessary in order to attain that inner stillness wherein you can hear the still, small Voice. If you must discipline yourself and sit in a corner for an hour at a time until you make this contact, it is worth the effort. To use scriptural language, if you must "pluck out your eyes or cut off your hands or feet" in order to attain that inner stillness, it is worth it! Nothing else in life is worthwhile. Do not believe for a moment that there is lasting satisfaction in building circles of friends or relatives or being successful in art, literature, finance, or music. There is lasting satisfaction only in the realization that "I and the Father are one and the Kingdom of God is within me. Christ, the Spirit of God, the Son of God, dwells in me; and I can tabernacle, I can commune, with this Father within." Then your life by Grace begins.

CHAPTER 5

LIVING THE MYSTICAL LIFE

The goal of the mystical life is for us to become beholders of God in action, where we ascribe nothing to ourselves—not even good motives. We no longer have desires. We no longer have needs because every need seems to be met before we are even aware of a need. This is called "living by Grace," but you can live fully by Grace only as that selfhood that has a desire, a hope, an ambition disappears. Then life is lived entirely by Grace, because *It* functions to its end, not yours or mine.

You see, if I prayed for something, it would mean I have a desire, an end, an object in life that I am seeking. But I have nothing to pray for. I have only this minute to live, this minute in which I must be fulfilled by the Spirit. If I have a tomorrow, it will be the same life, no matter whether it takes place here or in California, South Africa, or England. I will be there not because I desire to be there, but because I am sent. I do not desire to be any place except where I am sent. In that degree of desirelessness, selflessness, or unselfedness is the mystical life lived. That is what the mystical life is—attaining that degree of desirelessness in which every day you find yourself not wondering about tomorrow, because there is no tomorrow for you; there is only a tomorrow for God.

Even when God is living your life, God is a mystery. Who can fathom God? It is useless to try to fathom God with the mind. This takes us back to the beginning of this lesson of going beyond mind and thought.

When someone asks me for help, the first thing I do is stop thinking. I think no thoughts of Truth. I merely listen and let the Presence and Power of God through. The moment I try to think a thought, even of Truth or of The Infinite Way, I am trying to make thought a power, I am trying to make a statement of Truth a power. No statement or thought of Truth is God-power. Only God is God-power. So if you want God, be still and *let* God function. Otherwise, you are letting your ego in. What is worse, you are making graven images. Whether you build a wooden image and make it God-power or whether you put together a sentence and call it God-power or whether you take a thought and make it God-power, there is no difference. They are all graven images made by man. The only thing that is not made by man is what functions through man in the silence. That man has nothing to do with.

Any thought of God that is in your mind is a thought you created, and it is a graven image. Any word of God that is in your mind is a word you created. It is therefore a graven image. You must be absent from thought. Then whatever God is, and however It functions, takes place out there, and it is a miracle to human sense. But it is not a miracle that I performed, because this power is not mine. It is God's, and the more I refrain from thought and become a receptivity, the greater the Presence and Power comes through.

So, when I am asked for help, no matter what I am doing, all thought immediately stops, and whatever comes through is the Presence and Power of God, which does the work.

If you know in advance through the principles of The Infinite Way that no words or thoughts that go through your
mind will influence God, it will be easier for you to stop thinking words and thoughts and pray without them. But as long as
you believe that your words and thoughts will reach God and
influence Him, the more difficult it will be. However, the
sooner you realize that you are just wasting time, the sooner
your thoughts will come to a stop and your prayer will be a receptivity, a listening, an awaiting the still, small Voice. Then
the Spirit of God enters your consciousness, and you become
consciously aware of it.

When I am giving a class or when I am in meditation or
giving a treatment, at first there is a "me" listening for the still,
small Voice, a "me" inviting God to speak. Then as I get into
that listening attitude, this "me" disappears and there is only
the Presence fulfilling Itself. In periods of meditation when you
are no longer aware of the "you" of yourself, this will happen
to you, especially when the work is for others and for the world.
The "you" will disappear, and the Presence is all there will be.

This "pearl of great price" cannot be given to those who
have lived their entire lives by thought, by the intellect, by
the mind. When you tell beginners that God is present only
when all thought has been done away with, some become very
angry and insulted. So when you are imparting to beginners,
you must start by giving them the principles of The Infinite
Way as they are given in my writings until the students can be
carried further, step by step, until they are able to understand
and accept this fruitage of my nearly forty years of spiritual
searching.

When you become less concerned about what God is and
what The Infinite Way is, and as you gradually surrender yourself unto God, while at the same time using all the letters of
Truth and all the principles of The Infinite Way, then can you
lead those who come.

Truth Unveiled

The Infinite Way is a revelation of God revealing Himself on earth. Its purpose and its function is that you may "go and do likewise."

But there are do-gooders and egotists who "love" the Message so much that they go out into the world to spread the Message when they have not yet come into spiritual awareness and into the demonstration of their spiritual Selfhood. These do-gooders and egotists always get in the way of spiritual demonstration. Truth can be revealed only by Truth itself through the soul faculties, not by a human being through the mind. Therefore, when the do-gooders or egotists go out and start teaching Truth through the mind, they are preparing the generations for another period of the absence of God on earth. They always put the veil back on the revelations of Moses, Jesus, Isaiah, John, Paul, or Joel—or anybody else.

We can prevent this loss of Truth through the ministry of those who have not attained spiritual illumination by carefully selecting as a teacher one who shows the fourth-dimensional Consciousness and not one who merely has some knowledge picked up from a book. Let us be watchful, then, both when we are seeking a teacher and especially when we seek to teach.

Rising Above the Mind

When we rise above words and thoughts (the mind), we do not eliminate them. We simply are no longer living by them. When we rise above the mind, then, we are living by Grace. For example, in our metaphysical days we lived primarily by affirmations. We hoped to bring out harmony by our affirmations, by our words and thoughts and statements and remembrances of Truth. But in the days of the Sabbath and Grace, we no longer

live by words or thoughts, we no longer take words or thoughts
to live by. We are living by Grace.

The activity of Grace can come as words and thoughts that
I impart to you in words and thoughts. But I am not living by
those words or thoughts, and neither are you. I am living in the
Sabbath, resting from declaring words and thoughts. I am living by the Grace that produced those words and thoughts. I
am living by Grace, receiving the words and thoughts, being
filled with the Spirit of God, and letting them flow. I did not
think the words and thoughts; I did not make them up; I did
not arrange them. I simply let them flow from the Holy Ghost
through me. They are the thoughts and words of God that
make the earth melt, and they are coming through the teacher.

That Grace appears as the message you may speak or write.
Because it is a message of Grace, people hearing or reading the
Word are healed or have their lives transformed. This happens
again and again in our work.

The Revelation

The year of 1963 was another period of initiation for me. I had
no knowledge of the intensity of the initiation or its length or
the nature of the message that would be revealed. Living in two
worlds—living in that higher consciousness and then coming
back down to earth—has been difficult for me ever since my
first spiritual experience. But it was never before as difficult as
during that year. Therefore, it is not surprising that 1963 should
reveal a higher unfoldment, a higher consciousness.

The high point of this initiation period was the revelation
of "the nature of life as it is lived when we get beyond the mind
and thoughts"—beyond taking thought, beyond reasoning. In
this final step I experienced a revelation of the nature of Sabbath and of Grace. On the evening of Sunday September 1, a
revelation poured through me for two consecutive hours. I was

being led to the highest point of consciousness that the Infinite had revealed.

Throughout all my talks since this unfoldment, what has broken through has led to the message of going beyond words and thoughts—going beyond the mind.

Beyond Mind

It is only in our minds that we entertain the corporeal sense, and this "fleshly sense" of man cannot enter the Kingdom of Heaven, the Spirit. The middle path, or spiritual Consciousness, knows only the spiritual man—the Son of God. Melchizedek, Christ who was never born and will never die, is the true man. In our healing work we are unseeing or unknowing of the corporeal or physical sense of man—well or sick, rich or poor, good or bad—because there is neither. The corporeal sense is only our tempter. What we see, hear, taste, touch, and smell is our false sense of that man. You are not a false man or a fallen man or a physical man. We only entertain a false sense of the man you are! The healthy fleshly sense of man is as illusory as the sickly sense; the "good man" is as illusory as the "bad man." Therefore, in our work we do not engage in exchanging the sense of "erroneous man" to the sense of "correct man." Our healing Truth is our consciousness of incorporeal man and the universe.

Ascension

The ascension is always the same: a rising above mind, above knowing the Truth, to Truth Itself. In all of our classwork, probably even in the writings, I have said that I did not understand the crucifixion of Jesus or why, or even if, it had to take place. It was not until 1963, when I myself went through the

experience and the resurrection, that the reason for the crucifixion and the need for it was revealed to me. The memory of
that passed from me, and I could not bring it to conscious rec-
ollection. Later, when I went through the experience of ascension, the entire scene was again revealed to me. This is
what I saw.

Jesus reveals that He had attained the goal: *I Am, I Am
the Way. Thou seest me, thou seest God, for I and God are one.* He
proved it when He took three disciples to what is called the
Mount of Transfiguration (high Consciousness) and revealed to
them the Hebrew prophets who were supposed to have died.
In this way He proved that they are alive and that they are here
in form. It makes no difference whether He translated them
into visible form or whether He translated Himself and the disciples into invisible form, because it is the same experience.
Jesus proved that "I can lay down my life and pick it up. I can
walk into the invisible realm, and I can walk out again, for I am
Spirit, I am the Way."

Moses did not die. He did not know death. He was translated and entered the Promised Land, the invisible life of the
Spirit. Moses' followers were not aware of it because he was not
corporeally present with them as they continued on their journey. Enoch was translated without knowing death. Elijah was
translated without knowing death. Isaiah may have been translated without knowing death.

From this I know now that Jesus could have been translated without knowing death. He could have avoided being
crucified; but when Jesus became aware of the betrayal and un-
derwent trial and the threatened crucifixion, He chose to accept corporeal death in order to reveal to His disciples that
death is not an experience; it is an illusory sense we must see
through.

Jesus revealed that there is no such thing as death by per-
mitting Himself to experience corporeal death and by revealing

Himself in what appeared to be the same corporeal form with all its wounds. Having served that purpose, His continued presence on earth in corporeal form could only have been an embarrassment to the disciples, to the church, to Rome, and probably to Himself. Now we find that He is translated; He ascends out of corporeal form.

You can interpret this to mean that He rose above His own mind, because it is only in our minds that we entertain the corporeal sense, not in our spiritual faculties. In our soul faculties we are Spirit; we see each other spiritually, whether we are here on this plane or whether we are looking at those who have gone to the other plane or those who are not yet born.

Dying is not a condition that you actually go through. No one has ever died. There is no death. God has no pleasure in your dying and has never arranged for a death. Therefore, death is an experience only of corporeal sense, the sense that tells us we are physical, mortal, finite. Death is never an experience of our own being.

Becoming the Truth

We start on the spiritual path to learn Truth, study Truth, and practice Truth. Until we reach beyond the mind and its knowing the Truth, we can never attain the goal of realizing: *That which I am seeking, I Am.* When Moses spoke of himself as "being slow of speech," he still retained a finite sense of Moses. That finite sense of Moses could not enter the Promised Land. Until he could crucify that mortal sense of Moses that still remained, he could not enter the Promised Land, or heaven. On the Mount (high Consciousness), Moses realized the *I Am* and thereby became *I Am.*

All the Essenes knew the same truth, but Jesus realized Truth and *became* the Truth. Jesus retained a sense of Jesus when He stated, "I can of my own self do nothing. If I speak of myself, I bear witness to a lie." This sense of Jesus had to be crucified. Once He rose above the seeming mortal sense of self, he made the ascension. He became the Truth: *I am the Way. I am the Truth.* The ascension is always a rising above mind, above knowing the Truth, to Truth Itself.

The goal of The Infinite Way is to rise above the mind and attain the realization: *That which I am seeking, I Am.* Throughout my writings I have said again and again that I did not think up this message or invent it or create it. It was received, and always through listening—sometimes in periods of initiation, sometimes while giving lectures and classes, but always while in a state of receptivity. That state of receptivity is my hidden manna. It is what produces all that appears in this message.

In our teaching, we are feeding to the students all of these Words of God that have been revealed to us so that they can take them into their minds and bury them deep in their consciousness until they too rise above the level of the mind to where they can live without taking thought and be receptive to the still, small Voice. Never believe that The Infinite Way is teaching you to mentalize! Mentalizing is necessary only when you are learning Truth, when you are feeding your consciousness with the letter of Truth. We want no student to live by affirmations or denials, because that is not living by the Grace of God.

The Infinite Way message has been leading you to the stage where you live without words or thoughts. Keep working hard and long with the principles of The Infinite Way until the principles are embodied in you and your soul begins to feed you with the hidden manna. But do not make an eight-hour day of it. Take time out to work in your garden or read a good book or even read a good novel. You must learn to stop, sometimes for a day or two, and say, "Let me not trust my mind, let me relax in God." Invite the Soul! Relax in the Soul, without words or thoughts. God is not in the whirlwind. God is not in your problems. God is not in your thinking. God is not in your books. God is in the still, small Voice. In order to hear that Voice and receive Its impartations and Its Grace, we must live quietly and peacefully in the within.

There must come a rest from the activity of the mind, from taking thought for our lives, from fearing for our lives, from constantly knowing the Truth in order to avoid some experience. There must come a rest—the Sabbath. In this Sabbath we live by Grace, because now we do not merely know the Truth, we are Truth, and Truth reveals Itself to us. It is not an activity of our minds, it is the Soul revealing Itself. This period of rest is the fruitage of abiding in these principles. It is the true meaning of the Sabbath that Moses gave to the Hebrews. It was a period of rest forever.

Yes, labor for six days to know these principles until you come to the place where you realize, "'I' is God, and the Word that It imparts to me is the bread, the meat, the wine, and the water." Then you have entered the Sabbath, and for the rest of your days you live by the Grace of God, by my Spirit. When you reach that stage, you can relax and rest in the Truth instead of feverishly searching for and reading and studying Truth. You become a state of awareness without taking thought and without speaking or thinking and discover the meaning of "Man shall not live by bread alone but by every Word that proceedeth out of the mouth of God." Every word, every feeling, every emotion, every thought that comes to you from the deep withinness of you is what you now live by. It guides, it directs, it sustains, it protects. It goes before you to make the crooked places straight. Our ultimate goal must be to live in God, through God, and as God. Otherwise, how could the Master have revealed, "Take no thought for your life"? It is to be lived by every Word of God that we receive in our consciousness. There is always a sufficiency of God's Grace present for this moment. Therefore, we only have to be still in this moment to receive a sufficiency of Grace for this moment.

It takes a transcendental consciousness to unveil the Truth in the Bible. One must go beyond the words that have veiled the Truth. Everything in The Infinite Way is a spiritual interpretation of Scripture. It is not so much a teaching as it is an experience. It is intended to take you through the "five days" of labor: of thinking, of knowing the Truth, of searching for Truth, of pondering Truth, of meditating on Truth. Then it is intended to take you beyond words, thoughts, and activity of the mind or intellect so that you can rest in quietness and in confidence, knowing that you are no longer living your own life. Now every Word that flows from God into your awareness becomes the bread, the wine, the meat, and the water. Every Word becomes your health, strength, and vitality and all of those things that are necessary for your experience.

When you have transcended words and thoughts, you can go back into your own consciousness and draw out the spiritual interpretation of these Bible passages. Your interpretation of a passage may come in a form different than what I have given you, but the principle will be the same. Every time you go within, something new and fresh will come forth.

Self-Surrender

The period of Sabbath or Grace is the full and complete surrender of self. In all of us there remains a finite sense of self that in the last analysis must be crucified. Each of us has this personal sense of self when we believe we have (or do not have) a skill, a wisdom, or an art. Moses' sense of self was in his feeling of unworthiness. Jesus had it in his feeling of "I can of my own self do nothing." I definitely had it in the knowledge that I could not bring forth the message of The Infinite Way. That sense of self must be crucified until we can realize, "I do not have any Truth. I do not know Truth. I do not have any skill or art. I *am* the Truth, I *am* the art, I *am* the skill." In that moment, humanhood has "died" and Christhood has been "born" and revealed in its fullness, and the ascension or translation can take place.

It is never meant that we should glory in our wisdom, in our art, in our science, or in our skill. The reason we are on earth is to show forth God's glory. Therefore, we must recognize that what appears to the world as these is not really ours, but His. In other words, "All that the Father has is mine," and this glory is God's and this is what I am showing forth, not mine. Only God's Grace has raised up students, publishers, money, travel, and workers for The Infinite Way. The success and prosperity of The Infinite Way shows forth God's glory and God's Grace, not my prosperity or success. The message of The Infinite Way is God's message, not mine. No one knows better than I that The Infinite Way activity and message is Truth expressing Itself. It is God's Grace and glory being revealed in human consciousness. I, Joel, could never have done it! In your life—your activities, your business, your art, your profession— you too must realize that the nature of your experience is so that God may be glorified, that God may speak through you, or sing through you, or play through you, or act through you, or do business through you. Always, it is God functioning through and as your individual being.

The Sabbath is the complete surrender of self so that God may live on earth as He is living in Heaven. The two become one. There is no longer a man in heaven and a man on earth. The man who came down and the man who went up are one and the same. There is no longer a kingdom of heaven and a kingdom of earth; but the kingdom of heaven is made manifest on earth in oneness. Then it is in the realization that "I" (God) is individual consciousness (yours and mine). In that realization, we turn within. That is the function of meditation. I (Joel) turn within so that I (God) may reveal Itself through the Word to I (Joel) as long as there is an I (God) and an I (Joel). When I (God) and I (Joel) can sit in the same chair and commune with each other, that is getting very close to oneness. It is not as close as it will be some day when I ascend unto the Father, thereby becoming the Father.

Each Revelation Is a Specific Principle

The revelations that have been given to me appear in the message of The Infinite Way in specific form. Without revealing these experiences, I have given you the fruitage of them as specific principles, with instructions for embodying them, practicing them, and eventually living them. For example, the theme of an entire class in San Francisco was "My conscious oneness with God constitutes my oneness with all spiritual being and idea." This was incorporated into a book, *Conscious Union with God* (New York: University Books, 1962). If you were to study this book, you would understand that you have witnessed the demonstration of The Infinite Way. In other words, you would understand how one individual—alone with this message and without financial support, without organization, promotion or advertising, without attempting to draw anyone to this message, without seeking to draw any followers or requiring memberships or the payment of dues—could eventually carry this message around the world and witness it being published by many great publishing houses. The worldwide activity of The Infinite Way is the actual demonstration of the principle revealed in *Conscious Union with God*.

My conscious oneness with God has made me one with every one of you in any part of the world who has been drawn to this message. I have not humanly sought you out; I have not humanly proselyted or allowed anyone to proselyte for you. You who are studying the message of The Infinite Way, wherever you are on the face of the globe, have been drawn to this message and to me because my oneness with God has made me one with your spiritual identity, and we have become one.

In this same way, my conscious oneness with God has re-sulted in my oneness with all the funds necessary to conduct a worldwide activity, without my asking or pleading or taking up collections for funds. When literary agents could not suc-ceed in getting publishers for my books, my conscious oneness with God, the Source of all life, brought them forth. So in this experience of The Infinite Way you have actually witnessed the demonstration of that principle: *My conscious oneness with God constitutes my oneness with all spiritual being and idea.*

You will find the same kind of example in each one of my books. Each class brings forth some specific principle that leads us still another step toward our spiritual goal when we embody the principle in our consciousness. Very briefly, in 1956 karmic law was revealed and the Sermon on the Mount. In 1959 the letter of Truth as applied to spiritual healing was revealed: im-personalization and nothingization. In 1960 or 1961 the raising of the Christ in you was revealed. Step by step, these revela-tions were given to me. Then through classes and writings, I have given them to you. Each revelation must have brought about a greater spiritualization of your consciousness: the peel-ing off of the onion skin, the refining of consciousness, the pu-rification of consciousness. Each book, each class, each principle, when taken into our consciousness, has prepared us for the one ahead.

CHAPTER 6

THE INFINITE WAY CONCEPT OF GOD

Let us start with the realization that we do not know God. It is not always easy to admit this. When the inner unfoldment came to me that I did not know God, I remember I found it quite insulting. I thought I had a very good idea of God. When the Voice told me I did not know God, I was already in the healing ministry and was achieving some measure of success in it. But when the Voice tells you something, there is no use arguing with *It* because *It* knows best! There was only one thing to do, and that was to acknowledge that I did not know God aright.

So let us begin anew and admit that we do not know God. Let us ask ourselves, "How can I come into an understanding of the nature of God?" I cannot reveal it to you, and you cannot reveal it to me. In these past years, I may have had many wonderful experiences with God, and yet I cannot convey to you what God is. In your own experience, you may have marvelous experiences with God, actually coming face-to-face with God, but that will not enable you to tell someone else what God is.

In *The Oxford Book of English Mystical Work*, the revelations of English mystics, from the earliest to the most modern times, are given, showing how God revealed Himself or *Itself* to them and how they became acquainted with God and were able to be at peace forever after.

There is only one way we may be taught of God. Only God can reveal to us what He is, and each one must learn it from the Kingdom of God within himself or herself. In case you do not know why I say, "Turn within," let me refer you again to the Master, who tells us that the Kingdom of God is within you. Therefore, whatever it is that you seek, seek it within you or you will not find it. So we seek the Kingdom of God within ourselves; we seek within ourselves to understand the nature of God. We do this by turning within during our quiet periods of the day or night and speaking to God and asking Him, "God, reveal Thyself," just as the Master spoke to His Father within, and as Abraham spoke to God as friend. Like the Hebrew boy Samuel, we must turn within and say:

> Speak, Lord, thy servant heareth. I am listening, God. I am waiting for the revelation of Yourself from within my own being. The entire Kingdom of God is within me. God is closer than breathing and nearer than hands and feet. I accept that!
>
> I accept that the place whereon I stand is holy ground. I accept the teaching of the Master: "*I* will never leave you nor forsake you. *I* will be with you until the end of the world."
>
> I remember that You are ever with me and will never leave me or forsake me and will be with me until the end of time.
>
> Therefore, Thou art with me *now*, so speak, Lord, thy servant heareth. Reveal Thyself to me! Let me know thee as the Hebrew prophets of old knew Thee, as the Christian masters of old knew Thee, as the Oriental masters of old knew Thee, and as the modern mystics have known Thee.

Knowing God Aright

The only solution to the problems of the world is to know God aright, and you cannot know Him aright by merely thinking about God any more than I could be a musician by simply thinking about music. To become a musician, I would have to attain it some other way. And so it is with knowing God aright.

There are people who devote their entire lives to thinking about God, who live their lives with a Bible in their hands, and yet are nowhere near knowing God. All they have are the words in their minds, and those words are not God. God is not a word, and Christ is not a word. God is an experience. Christ is an experience. You can experience God, and you can experience Christ, but you can never know them aright with your mind. Even if the figure of Christ were to appear to you, it would be only the image of Christ that you hold in your mind. It would be only what you think Jesus Christ looks like, and such an appearance may be emotionally induced. Many people in Europe each year experience on their bodies the wounds of the Master, and the world treats them as if they were mystics. They are not! They are emotional neurotics who live so intensely with the picture of the Passion in their minds that eventually the picture externalizes itself on their bodies. As a matter of fact, you can bring out anything you want on your body if you live inside with the feeling of it long enough, because the mind and the body (matter) are one, and whatever you take into your mind must manifest itself on your body.

Knowing God aright is difficult at first, but eventually it must be attained by everybody by studying the message of The Infinite Way and practicing the principles. Then you must let the mind rest, because "the Bridegroom cometh only in the moment that ye think not." The Spirit—God, Christ—does not come when your mind is active, when you are exercising your intellect.

God Is

How could we possibly embrace the Allness of God with our little minds? Mainomides, the Hebrew mystic, wrote that when you say, "God is good, God is all power, God is all mighty, God is great," you are really only saying, "God *is*." The great Catholic mystic Julian of Norwich who wrote *The Cloud of Unknowing* said that when you say, "God is Love, or God is Divine Love, God is Omniscience," you are only saying, "God *is*."

Look out at your gardens and parks and ask yourself, "What produced that and how was it produced?" Look up at the sky at night and see the stars, the moon, the planets, ask yourself, "What produced them?" Does anyone know how this world came into being? As you look at our orderly universe of sun, moon, earth, planets, tides, and the nature that makes apples come from apple trees and peaches from peach trees, all you can say is, "Man did not create this; certainly I know that God *is*."

Having acknowledged that God *is*, you have gone as far as any deep religionist has ever gone. Going any further than this is setting the mind or the intellect to work, and this can only set up a barrier between yourself and God. But you can do something more than merely keeping it as a form of worship in the mind without setting up a barrier.

When you are realizing that God is not a word nor a thought but that God is Being, and you get back into silence where your mind is still and in quietness and in confidence say, "Speak, God, Thy servant heareth," you are acknowledging the infinite nature of God and his omnipresence and omniscience. What would you expect God to speak to you if not power, intelligence, Love? So in quietness and in confidence you say, "Speak, Lord," and listen for the still, small Voice. By doing so, you let God take over your life. You stop pretending that you are good or spiritual or charitable or benevolent, because we are charitable or benevolent or patient or loving only to the extent that we let God function through us. All else is pretense!

I make no pretense about Joel, and I make no claims for him. Those of you who have known me throughout my experience in this work know that I have never even claimed to have a good understanding. My understanding is completely limited to whatever comes through at the moment. Whatever I knew yesterday was yesterday's manna, which does me no good today. What comes through at this moment is not even my own understanding; it is God's gift to me and through me since, there is not God *and* me. It is God functioning *through* me. Moses, who was slow of speech, was told that he would not have to speak, that God would speak through him.

So give up your intellectual exercises of trying to know God with the mind or to worship Him with the mind, and live in the constant atmosphere of, "I live, yet not I. Christ liveth my life. God is my being." In the degree that you live in that atmosphere, you give up any pretense that you are accomplishing anything of your own self. Then there is no sense of personal attainment, there is no ego, there is no personal self.

It has been my particular saving grace that I have known from the beginning that The Infinite Way was a message that keeps coming through me from an invisible Source. If it were mine, it would have its limitations. It would have a beginning and an ending. But if The Infinite Way is God's message, then it is being expressed into human consciousness, and it will be there for eternity. The message must be from the true Source, because no one has ever been harmed or impoverished by The Infinite Way. Those who have been open and receptive and responsive to the message of The Infinite Way have been spiritually healed, physically or mentally or financially. Therefore it cannot be of man and must be of God; and since it is of God, Joel is responsible only for maintaining himself as a transparency today. He is not responsible for what happens to the message today or for what happens to it when he is no longer physically present, because that which sent it into expression will continue to function. No one is ever going to tamper with it. Never, never! It has no personal savior; it has no personal revelator. It is the Spirit of Truth Itself voicing Itself, and be assured that the voice of Truth will always have a transparency through which and as which to reach human consciousness.

God as Individual Being

You did not create your life. You did not even create your talents. So you must stop thinking of your individual life as yours and begin to think of it as God's life. God gave himself to this world as the begotten Son, you. God gave Himself to this world as you. He did not breathe your life into you; He breathed into you His life. It is His breath you are breathing; it is His life you are living; it is His mind you are functioning with. Your body is the temple of the living God, so the body you are functioning with is not even yours. It is His. The more you surrender yourself that God may function as your mind, your soul, your life, your breath, your being, your body, the more Divine Grace will be expressed as and through you. The ignorant may say that you are wonderful, noble, beautiful. But you, within yourself, will say to yourself, "How I wish you knew that this is not me you see but 'the Father who sent me,' for I and the Father are one." But this is true only when you have surrendered yourself to the extent that you are not trying to manipulate and influence God with your mind, not even in your behalf or your neighbor's behalf. It is true only when you accept God as the Being of every being and let Him function through you.

We must acknowledge God as the individual being of even our enemies. The longer we see them as human beings, the longer they will do something we must pray for and forgive.

There can be only one way to pray for our enemies, and that is to recognize God as their individual being. The more we realize this, the fewer mistakes they can make and the fewer sins they can commit. But the more we look upon them as sinning human beings whom we must forgive, the more egotistical we are and the more we bind them.

If I surrender myself to God and acknowledge that God is functioning through me, then I must acknowledge that whatever good is emanating from or through me is God and that whatever error appears is only my inability to let God fully function through me. If this is true of me, then it must be true of everybody, whether they are aware of it or not. How can they be made aware of it? Not through themselves, because the human mind that is functioning them will not give itself up. They become aware of it only when the Christ has touched them.

So it has been with you, and so it has been with me. We became aware only after we were touched by the Spirit at some time in our lives. In our humanhood, we would have gone on forever in our paganistic orthodoxy or in our mental abracadabra. We could not have taken ourselves away from our humanhood because it meant abandoning the faith of our fathers, abandoning the friends and relationships we had developed, and attaining a secret life within, hidden from our friends and relatives. As humans we did not have that capacity any more than our human friends have. We could do so because we were touched by the Spirit. It may have happened when we at some moment in our experience just opened ourselves, or it may have happened when someone else's praying reached our consciousness. It could have happened when a mystic on the other side of the Veil prayed for us, because the mystics are not dead; they are spiritually alive and in our consciousness. So it could have been their prayers that reached us, or it could have been the prayers of a mother, a grandmother, or a great-grandmother still praying in what we call the beyond that touched us.

We do not know where the Spark came from that made us "leave our nets." Remember that we have left our nets in the degree that we have left our old mortality, in the degree that we have left the church of our fathers, in the degree that we have let friends and relatives drift out of our lives. Please believe that you could not have done so of yourself. If you could have, then everyone else in the world would be doing so, because you may be assured that they want what we have: the peace of mind, the peace of soul, a healthier physical body, a more intelligent mind. They want a greater assurance of God's Grace in the world, because they live in a horrible fear of bombs and wars, which would drop away if they had assurance of God's Grace. They want what we have, but they do not have the capacity until they have been touched by the Spirit. Until then, they have no knowledge of how we attained what we have, and the way we attained it seems monotonous, dull, and dreary to them and they do not want to go that way. They do not have the capacity until a Spark touches them. That Spark may come through our prayers or through the meditation and prayers of those in monasteries or nunneries or on the other side of the veil.

Once you have been touched by the Spirit and are on this path, you can never again be thrilled by the profits of the pocketbook or the things of the flesh or by what you once thought were pleasures. Once a person is touched, these pleasures and profits can only be incidental. However, there is still the possibility of turning back and fearing the things that we have always feared.

Evaluating One's Spiritual Progress

There is a way of evaluating what degree of progress we are making on the spiritual path. It is not by noticing how much more spiritual we feel or how better we are behaving or how much more virtuous we are. These are not the signs. We can evaluate our spiritual progress by our reactions to what is presented to us in the pictures of the world. For example, the more we realize that temporal power is not power, the less we fear war or the threat of war. That is one sign of spiritual progress. Another is reacting with less horror or fear to the sins and diseases of the world. You also show your own spiritual progress as you realize that supply is spiritual and react with less horror or pity to the seeming lack of food and necessities in the impoverished countries of the world. You not only show your progress, you also help to remove lack and limitation.

The last enemy to overcome is death, which may be only a fear of the unknown. At some time or other, we must overcome the fear of death by realizing that it is not actually death. It is a transition into a different state of experience. Regardless of what the appearance may be, we do not die. We simply make a transition into another phase of life, much like a larva becomes transformed into a butterfly.

One cannot remain a child forever, and thus we all have to face the fact of becoming a youth. As wonderful as that phase may be, we then must face the realities and responsibilities of adulthood. Adulthood coming to an end may be the most difficult period for some. The children marry and have families of their own, and we parents become onlookers in their lives. Some parents never make the transition into this phase of life and continue to meddle in the lives of their children and grandchildren, making everyone miserable. If we are to be really mature, we must acknowledge that the time has come when our children's lives are their own and we must make a separate life for ourselves.

Then we must face the fact that we have to leave that phase of life and enter another. That phase is the one we know the least about. But if you face death and lose your fear of it, you are wholly on the spiritual path, because you will have realized that you have no selfhood, that God is your Selfhood, that the life you are living is God's, that it is God living your life, and that you are perfectly willing for God to take it around the world or even into the next world. Once you have lost your fear of death, you are wholly on the spiritual path.

CHAPTER 7

GOD, THE SOURCE AND SUBSTANCE

Regardless of the degree of spiritual consciousness we have, some around us may not respond. Even the Master, Christ Jesus, could not avoid his Judas, or his doubting Thomas, or his denying Peter, or his disciples asleep in the garden. Peter eventually awakened and undoubtedly atoned in a measure, and probably Thomas did as well. Of Judas's eventual awakening to the spiritual Light we have no record. We do know there must have been a time when Saul of Tarsus could not respond to this spiritual impetus, yet eventually at a certain moment he not only responded to it but he also became a living witness to it.

There are moments in the lives of many when they cannot respond to the spiritual influence that is about them. But eventually they will respond, in their time. With some it may take days, weeks, months, or years. With others it may take many lifetimes. But sooner or later, at some time, every knee will bend—every knee! So we need not despair if we find some in our families, in our church groups, or in our national or international life who are not at this moment responding to the spiritual impulse.

That brings us to a very important point. In our experience, we are apt to believe that we are being held back by the lack of demonstration on the part of someone around us or that, for one reason or another, their lack of demonstration may be having an adverse influence on us. That would be true only in the degree that we permit it. If we are not yet ready to leave those who are holding back our demonstration, the blame is ours for clinging to the universal belief that our good comes from others or that their good comes from us. To understand how and why this is so, you need to know your true identity and your relationship to God.

Your True Identity and Your Relationship to God

The Master Jesus tells us that in order to attain the heights of Christhood, we must leave mother, father, brother, and sister for His sake. We must leave our nets, and many of us have not yet done so. Actually, except for rare cases where husbands must leave their wives, or wives must leave their husbands for the sake of their freedom, we need not physically leave mother, father, sister, brother, wife, or husband if we understand our relationship to God and our relationship to each other.

In the fifteenth chapter of John, we learn that we are the branch: "I am the Vine, and the Father is the husbandman." Let us consider a tree. Note its branches and its trunk and visualize its underground roots. Choose one particular branch on that tree and note its connection to the trunk of the tree. Follow the trunk down into the ground and visualize its connection to the roots and the surrounding earth from which the tree gets its sustenance. The branch is supported and sustained by the roots and the earth through the trunk that connects them. Even if all the other branches were sawed off, the branch would still maintain its permanence, its life, its fruitfulness.

Now look at the other branches on the same tree. Not one branch contributes to the other branches. Each branch has its existence independently of the other branches. If one branch were to complain that another branch is not sharing or cooperating, you would see how ridiculous that would be. You would say to the complaining branch, "How can you be concerned about the other branch's actions when you yourself are connected to the trunk and the roots in the ground from which you get your sustenance?" That is the truth of the branch's being.

The Master tells us that our relationship to God is like that of a branch. Each of us is a branch, Christ is the Vine, and God is the Substance. Start realizing that you are the branch and that God is your only substance and sustenance. Your sole responsibility is to maintain your contact with your Source through the Vine, and you will flourish and bear fruit richly. Your good is from your Source, not from other branches. They are not responsible for you, and you are not responsible for them! Each branch has its own contact with its source. Therefore, no other branch can have an adverse influence on another; no branch can have a conflicting or destructive effect on the other.

Of course, if you *want* to be dependent on a practitioner for your support or for your treatment, then you make yourself dependent on the practitioner, and it this dependency that interferes with your demonstration. If you accept the universal belief that your source of supply or health is your husband or wife or investments or business, you permit yourself to be influenced by them. They indirectly affect your demonstration, but you can blame only yourself for clinging to this dependency.

We can live together with our families and yet maintain the integrity of our contact with our Source and never become dependent upon the other for anything. Certainly we can live with each other harmoniously, cooperate with each other, and

share with each other. But are we sharing from our own resources? No, we are sharing from the Source, God. Whatever
we share with one another was never ours, because "The earth
is the Lord's and the fullness thereof." Whatever we share is
from the infinite bounty of God. Any limitation comes only
when we claim that we are sharing something that is ours. If
you realize that anything you give or share never was yours
and if you have no personal sense of glory about sharing or giving since it came from the Source, it will never run dry. The
Source, which is God, never runs dry! It is infinite!

There is another lesson to be learned from the fifteenth
chapter of John: "Every branch that beareth not fruit, the
Father purgeth." That is the branch that lives unto itself and
thinks of itself as separate and apart from the Vine and the
Husbandman. It is the branch that thinks it has its own wisdom, its own supply, which it is sharing or else is not sharing for
fear of a lack. That branch is ultimately purged.

That brings us to the two commandments: "Thou shalt
have no other Gods before me" and "Love thy neighbor as thyself." Until you acknowledge God as your only Source, as your
infinite Source, and love thy neighbor as thyself, you are the
branch that is trying to live unto itself, trying to draw its
fruitage out of its little branchhood. It ultimately finds itself
running dry and then being purged. The only way to understand and to demonstrate life eternal is to understand God as
the Source of all being. We do not make this true; it already *is*
true. If we are not experiencing limitless fruitage, it is only because we have not yet acknowledged it as Truth and opened
ourselves to that flow. Whatever happens in our experience is
the result of an activity in our own consciousness. The moment
we open our consciousness and realize our relationship with the
Vine and the Husbandman, the flow begins. In the same way,
when we withdraw our labels from God and live only with
"God Is," then God fills us with *Its* Truth, and that Truth is

our meat, our bread, our wine, our water, and life eternal. It is the Source of our unending and limitless supply. It is an activity of consciousness.

The story of David and Goliath in the Bible illustrates the power of the powerless, the power which is not power. Goliath was a giant clad in armor that no power could penetrate. He was so well armored that he was invincible from any weapon that had been conceived or made at that time, at least any weapon on the outer plane. Then along came David with only a few pebbles, and it took only one of those tiny pebbles to end the career of the mighty Goliath clothed in his heavy armor! The thought that a little pebble could level a giant clothed in armor from head to foot is fantastic. But David said, "I come to you in the name of God." That is the secret; that is the miracle! "I do not come to you with physical power or physical might. I do not come with a weapon stronger than yours. I come to you in the name of God."

The Master gives us a correlative story. When His disciples came to Him, so proud that they had been given the power over the devil, He rebuked them. "Oh, no! The devils are not subject unto you. Just be grateful your names are writ in heaven. That's all. Nothing is subject unto you. Just, your names are writ in heaven." What does that mean, your names are writ in heaven and the devils are not subject unto you? It means that there is no power other than God's. You have no power, the devils have no power. Do you see how we always come back to the basis of The Infinite Way? We stand in the name and in the nature of God. That is why there is no weapon formed against us that can prosper, not because we have any weapons over the devil, but just because we stand in the name and in the nature of God. Let us see that at work.

If I were to acknowledge that any person or other influence or power on earth could be destructive, to me in any way, I would need some form of defense, some form of power, against it. But I have the mightiest one: the realization that there is no power other than the name and nature of God. There is no destructive influence unless God be the destructive influence to any concept unlike itself. The God-realization in me reveals that nothing in the world of effects, concepts, or persons is an evil power. Therefore, I need nothing with which to overcome evil. Observe this in your own lives. When some threat comes to your person, whether from an individual, or armies, or bombs, stand fast in the name and nature of God, in the realization that no weapon or concept that is formed has power over the Truth of being, and see what happens.

The same applies to your healing work. If you have accepted the belief in infectious and contagious disease, inherited disease, or any other form of disease, watch what happens when you give up your mental weapons and stop fighting disease and the causes of disease. Realize that you stand in the name and nature of God and that there is no weapon, no belief, no concept of man that can stand in opposition to the name and nature of God. Why? The story of David and Goliath tells us that the battle is the Lord's, not yours, not mine. We need no physical or mental powers. A little pebble, the least of them, is sufficient to tear down the stronghold of the mighty Goliath. A tiny little stone, a nothingness, that to us represents no power at all can overthrow the mightiest power when that power is physical or mental. Spiritual power is a self-maintained, self-created, and a self-sustained power. All you have to do is stand in its name and nature and let yourself be clothed in this spiritual armor of Truth. But do not use this spiritual armor of Truth as a weapon against error! Let God be *Its* own defense.

Let us stand clad in the armor of the Spirit, and we will never find injustice against us. The law is a fine thing, but it is wrong for those who come to a higher level of living by the Spirit to use man's weapons. Some years ago, I became involved in a lawsuit. I had been assured by attorneys and judges that I had a moral right to a small sum of money and that if I did not take it to court I would be very foolish and would be letting my substance be taken from me. This small sum of money was all that I had. I heard the still, small Voice say to me, "Those who live by the sword will die by the sword." It came in such a way that I understood that I had no right to go to the law. But I listened to others who convinced me that I had to defend my rights. In spite of hearing for the second time, "Those who live by the sword will die by the sword." I let my friends prevail against God and I went to court. It was a sad and pitiful experience! Not only did I lose the case and the lawyers' fees, but my reputation suffered as well. I know now that I would have suffered no injustice had I not brought it on myself by going to court. It was a hard lesson, but I learned it well!

There is a lesson in this not only for me but also for all of our Infinite Way students. If it is at all possible to avoid using the weapons of the world, do so, and have full confidence that the battle is the Lord's and not yours. We may at times resort to the use of medicines and surgery, and all of us have fallen down in that respect and we probably will again. These are temporary experiences. But as a principle by which to live, we must not be induced to use the weapons of the world, but stand in the name and nature of God for our defense.

The Practitioner as Vine

Too many people believe that their help comes from the practitioner or from studying books or from attending lectures and classes. What you learn from books, lectures, or classes are merely stepping stones, so do not look to them for your spiritual harmony because that is not where it comes from. The Source is the Kingdom of God within your own being. Therefore, seek ye the knowledge of God, the wisdom of God, the activity of God within your own being—closer to you than breathing, nearer than hands and feet. No one can retard your demonstration, not even a practitioner who lacks understanding, because your healing comes *through* the practitioner and not *from* the practitioner. Even the Master Christ Jesus said, "The Father doeth the work. I can of my own self do nothing." Never did He lead us to believe that He was the source of good. He was only the Vine, and God the Father was the Husbandman who fed us through the Vine.

The practitioner functions as the vine. God's love flows through the practitioner to the patient. The teacher functions as the vine to the student. But the Source is God, the Husbandman. At this moment you are the branches, and I am the vine. What is going out to you is coming from the Father through me to you. Therefore, I am functioning as the vine. But when you leave this class, you become the vine to your family, your friends, your relatives, your business associates, and the world at large. Every time we function as a practitioner or as a teacher, we function as a vine unto the branches. When we are alone, we again are the branch, and the Vine is the invisible Presence within us that we call the Christ. But the Father is *always* the Source from which universal good flows.

That is why I say that it is not the love or understanding of your practitioner that will help you. It is the love and understanding of God, flowing through your practitioner as the vine, that will help you. When you function as teacher or practitioner, it is not your love and understanding that will help anyone. It is God's Love. You are merely the avenue through which it flows. We are all only instruments used by the Father to show forth His glory and His Grace.

We Are Only Instruments

God is the revelator, the actor, the doer, the be-er. It is God who knows, understands, imparts, and receives. God is the only activity. Therefore, we can be only the instrument for God's work, God's labor, and God's Love; the only success there can be is God's success, not ours. "I can of my own self do nothing. The Father does the work."

In our religious world, we travel from point to point in consciousness. Sometimes we believe that we have arrived at the ultimate point. On this path again and again we have the conviction, "This is it! Now I know what it's all about. Now I understand these things for which I have been searching and seeking." If we are really wise, this sense of satisfaction will not last long—anywhere from a day to a month—before we realize, "No! There is another point beyond this."

In the old days, it was said that I was always seeking new horizons. I never really sought a new horizon; they were always opening up to me. Each time I thought, "Oh, if I catch this final point, then all things will be opened unto me." I would catch a glimpse of it and actually feel, "This is it! Now I am home; now I am in heaven! Never again will a problem arise that cannot be met instantly because now I know all things." For two or three days I was happy in that realization, then another horizon would appear: one more degree of understanding, the last veil that would fall away. All my energy and desires would then be concentrated toward that one last point. "Just let me get to *this* horizon, and there heaven will be spread out."

Again and again, I had the feeling of really and truly having arrived at understanding only to find that there was still one more point. Evidently, even that was not Truth, because one day a new sensation came to me which "threw" me. I suddenly realized that I knew nothing about Truth, that everything I had heretofore believed was not Truth at all! Somehow or other I had either missed the way or been self-deceived or had judged from appearances. Appearances rarely testify to Truth, especially in religious unfoldment. It is true that I had had a healing here or there, someone else had had a healing, or supply had been increased a bit, or someone else's employment problem had been met. All of these appearances were tempting me to believe that I had found the Kingdom of Heaven. I did not recognize the symptoms then; now I do.

The Master commanded His disciples, "Leave your nets!" We had not been leaving our nets. We were not leaving our sense of human good. We were not leaving our channels of good. What we had been seeking was more fish to fill our nets—more fish, more supply, more health, more of the human good. Some of us were desperately trying to be good; others were desperately trying to be healthy or to find employment. We were seeking more fish for our nets, not for what might happen once we left those nets.

The day came when I realized, "I'm all wrong. I have been on the wrong path. I'm not blaming anyone or the teaching. The teaching isn't wrong; only my understanding of the teaching has been wrong." There was an emptying out, and I made a new beginning. A new concept came. To all appearances, I did beautifully with it, and things seemed to be working out wonderfully well. Then one day came the realization, "I've made the same mistake again! What I thought was Truth is not." I went through that process several times. The latest one was terrible. It lasted three days, and I went through about as much hell as one man can take. Finally, the thought came, "Admit it! You are a failure! You have failed in everything you have undertaken since you started on this path. Here and there a few people seemed to get well, a few people have written they have been lifted up, but that is not success. Nothing real has been accomplished in your life. If you were to pass from this scene today what could you say was your accomplishment? At most, a few people healed who might have been healed by *materia medica* anyhow, a few lives prolonged a bit. But that is not a worthwhile achievement at all! That is not a life's work! That does not even pay your mother for the birth pains. Admit it, you are a failure!"

I went to my desk and began an entry in my notebook. I wrote, "This finishes my career in Truth. I know now how I

have failed. In some way I have missed the way. There isn't
even a hope of any success." I wrote page after page. Finally, the
thought came to me, "Yes, but there is a God, and you owe Him
something just for the privilege of having lived. How can you
say thanks to God?"

The thought came, "Well, God, this is a failure. No doubt
about that! But look what a grand and glorious failure! I have
spent thirty years getting to this point of failure. I've really
given my heart, my soul, my energy, every ounce of me to this
failure! So if that is all I have to offer, take this: a failure, but I
am so proud of it because I gave myself wholly unto it. Take
my failure and be glad that one of your children could work this
hard and have as big a failure! I'm sure it is the biggest on
earth!" A great sense of relief and peace came to me, and with
that sense of peace came this message.

Never have you understood more truly. You have
failed, of that there can be no doubt. But there never was
a chance for success in your experience! From the very
beginning, you never had a chance to make a success of
this. You were doomed to failure from the very beginning.
The more you realize that, the closer you will come to
Truth.

That was astonishing! Now it was evident that my failure
was in *believing* that I had the power to succeed or fail, when
all I could ever be was an instrument for the power of the
Divine. God alone is the principle of life. The only success that
can come in this world is God's success.

Thus, born in one night after many weeks of toil and sor-
row, began a new ministry with the conviction that I never can
have a success nor can I have a failure. The earth shows forth
His handiwork, and the heavens declare His glory. Can you
imagine the heavens or the earth being successful or failing?
The heavens and the earth are only the instruments for showing forth an activity of the Divine.

That is what has drawn us together, and we are here for the purpose of becoming instruments for showing forth God's activity. We are gathered together to share this inspiration, to partake of this same meat, to drink of this same wine or water. Give up once and for all the belief that you can succeed or fail in understanding Truth! You *will* succeed because you will forever and forever show forth God's handiwork by forever being the consciousness where God shines through. The glory of our being is not the glory of our being; it is the glory of God's Being. Do you see now why the great masters of all times have revealed that humility is the beginning point of wisdom. Humility is not depreciating one's self. True humility is the realization of God's Allness. It is knowing one's self as that which shows forth the full and complete glory of God. The light of God is our light. The wisdom of God is our wisdom. The love of God is our love.

The principle of humility is clearly shown in my booklet *Love and Gratitude*. There you will find how foolish and unwise it is to look to any man or any woman for justice, mercy, kindness, fairness, love, wisdom, or consideration. We learn to look to God for these things and, as we do so, we find all men to be instruments of them. True, along the way here and there we may find a Judas or a Peter or a Thomas. Sometimes we may find some of our friends or relatives asleep, not supporting or upholding us. That is of no consequence to you or to me, and that is a major point. It makes no difference in your life or mine who fails you. It does make a difference to those who fail you because they have failed in their demonstration of their Christhood. But it is of no consequence to you because you have no demonstration to make that is dependent on anyone on earth. You have learned your true relationship to God, and God has become the life, wisdom, activity, and supply of your being. You are spiritually fed, clothed, and housed. Your complete reliance is on the Truth that "all that the Father has is mine." If this entire earth were wiped away, you and the Father would still be one, and all that the Father has would still be yours.

That is your relationship to God, and that is God's relationship to you. That relationship has nothing to do with your relationship to others—whether it is to me or to your relatives, friends, or associates. Your good has nothing to do with them, and their good has nothing to do with you. The only relationship you have with each other is one of friendship, joy, and cooperation. It is never one of dependence, not even the human dependence of wife and husband, children and parents. In the outer picture it may well be that our income is derived from our employment, investments, husband, wife, child, or parent. We would suffer if these relationships were wiped away, but we would not lose our relationship of joint heir with Christ in God. The human picture does not testify to that, because there is a missing link. "Ye shall know the truth, and the truth shall make you free."

To benefit by the relationship of Father and Son, an activity of Truth must take place in your consciousness—in *your* consciousness, not in someone else's consciousness for you, because that would be only a temporary help. Sooner or later, every individual must open his or her own consciousness to the truth of being. Truth must become active in your consciousness so that from morning to night, and night to morning, you consciously acknowledge:

—Thank you, Father! I am the instrument of Thy being. I am that place where the fullness of the glory of the Godhead shines through. I have no wisdom of my own, I have no age of my own, I have no body of my own, I have no soul of my own. I have no goodness of my own. There is but one good: the Father in heaven.

As we realize that our good comes from the Father, that good becomes the health, wealth, harmony, joy, peace, activity, youth, vitality of the Son. But this Truth must be active in your consciousness. Demonstrating freedom in Truth is an individual thing (as is any demonstration). Because it is an individual thing, there can be no such thing as mass salvation. That is why we do not go out on a street corner or hire a baseball park or a football field or an arena or a stadium to give this message to twenty thousand people. They would be looking only for some magic statement of Truth or for a piece of marble to hold in their hands or for quotations to dream about in the hope that these things would make their demonstration.

CHAPTER 8

MESSAGE TO TEACHERS ON
THE SPIRITUAL PATH

The ministry of Truth tempts many to enter the path to gratify their ego in being known as a practitioner or teacher or lecturer or leader or for some other desire for personal gratification. Be sure you have received the signal within, which is your passport on the journey. The greatest temptation above all others is having one's own concept of Truth. Complete discipleship comes only when all sense of personal knowledge of Truth disappears.

While we are on earth, there is never a time when we are outside the range of temptation, because temptation is subtle. It can appear as the desire for prestige, wealth, or fame, or it can appear as the temptation to wield power. Once an individual has been touched by the Spirit, people believe that is not possible for them to sin. That is not true! The Bible is filled with those who succumbed to temptation. There was Judas. There was Lot's wife. There was Peter, who denied the Master. Even Jesus was tempted three times, although He did not succumb to these temptations.

The person on the spiritual path, even if he is at the beginner's level, should become conscious of the fact that a wrong done by him or her is far more serious than a wrong done by others. *A wrong done under the robe of the Spirit is a crime against the Spirit.* There is only one Consciousness, so once God Consciousness has become the consciousness of the teacher and the teacher violates that God Consciousness, the penalty is great. That teacher loses the God Consciousness. It is of utmost importance, therefore, that everyone on the spiritual path, but especially those who would be teachers, maintain at all times a high degree of spiritual integrity.

Coming into an Awareness of Spirit

Healing work cannot be done with the mind, just as God cannot be reached through the mind. If you knew all the truth in metaphysical textbooks such as *Science & Health with Key to the Scriptures* by Mary Baker Eddy, or *Lessons in Truth* by H. Emilie Cady (Unity Village, Mo.: Unity School, 1903) or *The Infinite Way*, you still could not heal, because healing is not done by knowledge. It is not done by formula, neither is it done by statements of Truth. No matter how much you know about the letter of Truth, it will do very little for you unless you have attained a measure of spiritual consciousness.

The principles of healing that constitute the message of The Infinite Way can be found throughout my writings. So if you have been learning and practicing the principles, you have at the same time been developing the spiritual consciousness necessary to make those principles operate. I can also say that those of you who have studied Christian Science, or Unity, or Divine Science, or one of the authentic New Thought teachings have also developed your spiritual consciousness sufficiently to take The Infinite Way principles and work with them understandingly. In my book *Living the Infinite Way* (New York: Harper & Row, 1961), you will find a great deal on developing spiritual consciousness. Here is a passage from that book:

> One of the greatest spiritual teachers who ever walked this earth has told us that man does not live by bread alone but by every word that proceedeth out of the mouth of God. . . . The Word becomes the living waters. It is our protection, our safety, our security. As we go about our tasks and duties, even though we may go through deep waters and be tried in the fire of experience, the waters will not overflow us and the flames will not kindle upon us if the word of God is in us and with us. . . . We must understand that the message of The Infinite Way is not to give the world a new teaching, but to give the world an experience. The Infinite Way is actually a God-experience, a Christ-experience. The Infinite Way is not in its writings, lectures, or classes. These are but instruments leading us to The Infinite Way, and The Infinite Way itself is the God-experience. (pp. 9–10,12)

An intellectual knowledge of Truth is of no benefit to us in developing our spiritual life or developing our eternality and immortality, neither is it of benefit in bringing health to this physical frame. Only as we are spiritually attuned to the center of our being (which is God), only as we are in attunement with the Source of life, in that proportion are we fed by the waters of life, by the bread of life, which is every word that proceeds out of the mouth of God. Without spiritual discernment, none of this is possible.

Inner Attunement

Anyone can read Scripture or metaphysics textbooks, but only those who have received some measure of inner illumination, some measure of inner attunement, can heal. Therefore, our major work is developing inner attunement. Then, when we have the correct letter of Truth along with it, we can do healing work. It can work either way. It is possible to first become spiritually illumined and then learn the correct letter of Truth. Or, it is possible to work faithfully with the correct letter of Truth (by building on it and practicing with it) and then develop one's self spiritually. But here one must be careful, because *not everything that is published as truth is Truth.*

There is a reason for this, which probably would take far too long to explain completely, but I will tell you this. Beyond the physical, there are two levels of consciousness: the mental and the spiritual. In the earliest days of introspection, many people turned inward and touched the mental realm. Because it was something greater than what they had ever known, they thought they had reached the Kingdom of God.

That was Mr. Quimby's primal mistake. He touched the mental realm and dressed it up by calling it "God," "Christ," "Spirit" and "prayer." He was really responsible for much of the mistaken teachings in the world.

Mrs. Eddy took Mr. Quimby's mental teaching and in the same way embroidered her message with the same names. In her mental teachings, she states that sin, ignorance, and fear are the procuring causes of all diseases. She did not go beyond this mental teaching until many, many years later. In her spiritual teachings she says that neither disease itself, nor sin, nor fear has the power to cause disease or relapse.

In other words, in the mental realm, you find mental cause for disease. Whenever you stop at the mental level and believe that you have attained the Kingdom of God, you are indulging in a false Christ. The Master Jesus warned us that there would be "false Christs come in My name."

You can always recognize one from the other because in the mental realm there are two powers: good and evil. You can do good with your mind, and you can do evil with your mind. But in the spiritual realm, there is neither good nor evil. There is only God, the Spirit, which is perfection, wholeness, completeness, and harmony. In the spiritual realm, you do not even have one power, for there is no need of power. God alone *is*, and there is not anything to use a power on, for, or against.

Be assured that as long as you are playing around with mental causes or reasons for physical disease or poverty, you will never develop your spiritual consciousness.

Developing Spiritual Consciousness

To develop your spiritual consciousness, you have to work with a spiritual principle that is based entirely on God as Spirit and entirely on the revelation that what appears to us as sin, disease, and death (or even the mental causes for those) are illusions, are without foundation, and have no law of God to support them. You have to work with a principle in which you learn to live and move and have your being in one: one Life, one Soul, one Spirit, one Law. Then you can realize, "This world can have no power over me. Only the Power which is of God has power over me." In that way you can develop the very spiritual consciousness that brings about healing.

These principles are presented clearly, simply, and concisely in my 1959 classes. Any two, or all, of the 1959 Hawaiian Village classes, the 1959 San Diego classes, the 1959 London classes, the 1959 Manchester classes, or the 1959 New York classes will give you these principles and their application in treatment. You can study them and work with them for the development of your spiritual consciousness.

These principles have been extracted from all my writings and my tape recordings and are presented in my books *The Art of Spiritual Healing* (New York: Harper & Row, 1959) and *The Infinite Way Letters—1959* (Marina del Rey, Ca.: DeVorss, 1990), and particularly the months of June, September, October, and November 1959 issues of The Infinite Way monthly *Letters*. The principles stand out clearly so that you cannot miss them and you can put them into practice.

I suggest that when working with the tape recordings of my classes, be sure to include some of the 1959 classes. These recordings will bring you far along in learning these principles and how to apply them and, through their practice, will bring forth healing fruitage.

All serious students can be healers in whatever degree they themselves determine, but only those whom God has led to the study of a spiritual and metaphysical teaching. The others are not yet ready to read and understand what they read, and they are definitely not ready to devote the necessary time and effort to the practice.

But those like you who have been led to such a message as this and have spent years studying and now devote days, weeks, and months to the practice of the principles of The Infinite Way must develop a healing consciousness. The degree of healing consciousness will depend on how much time and effort you devote to reading, meditating, pondering, and treating.

In the beginning, you may give thousands of treatments and not see enough fruitage to warrant your continuing, but that happens to all of us. We all have to go through difficult days until we become so immersed in the Spirit and the Spirit in us and the principle so certain that we never lift our thoughts to fighting an evil or a discord. Until we never strive to overcome or remove a condition. Until with every erroneous appearance that is presented to us, we immediately have an inner recognition that the carnal mind is not Power, that what is not of God is not Power, that what does not emanate from God has no Law of God to sustain it. But remember that merely declaring this Truth will not make it so. Only as this Truth becomes so much a part of you that it is your very consciousness will it then become so.

Wherever you find a consistently good healing practitioner, remember it is because of his or her degree of evolved spiritual consciousness. The Master Jesus was the greatest healer because He had the greatest degree of evolved spiritual consciousness. If a practitioner could rise to the absolute zenith of Christ-consciousness, the chances are that few, if any, would be left unhealed. But no one can heal everybody who seeks healing. It takes years and years to understand why all of us are not healed of all of our troubles all of the time.

Spiritual Discernment

Unless you have spiritual discernment, words are meaningless. You must therefore develop your spiritual discernment so that you will instinctively and automatically know the meaning of esoteric language.*

For example, the word *within* does not mean within something. It does not mean within the body. Before the Master Jesus used the word *within*, God was thought of as being in heaven, up on a cloud where Moses went. God was thought of as something to be attained or discovered or reached on a holy mountain or in a holy temple. The Master Jesus used the word *within* to bring God down from the clouds and make God closer to you than breathing and nearer than hands and feet, and yet not inside your body. Solomon said that as big and as wonderful and as holy and as dedicated as his great temple in Jerusalem was, it could not contain God. Now, then, how can your body contain God? So, we can only understand the word *within* to mean within and without, up or down, filling all space, not confined or localized, and yet not separate and apart from us.

A second example: "There is a sin unto death" (2 John 5:16). Is there an unforgivable sin? In the Hebrew teachings,

*Editor's note: the dictionary defines *esoteric* as "designed for and understood by the specially initiated alone. Knowledge that is restricted to a small circle."

there are two unforgivable sins: murder and adultery. Moses killed a man, yet he became the leader of the Hebrews, their liberator, their savior. Evidently, God forgave Moses, or Moses would never have attained that height. To the woman taken in adultery, the Master Jesus said, "Neither do I condemn thee." I can assure you that if those two sins were forgiven by God, then there is no unforgivable sin!

A third example: "The soul that sinneth, it shall die" (Ezekiel 18:4). Is it possible for a soul to die? Do you not see that it is all a matter of semantics? Then to what do these Bible references have meaning? They have meaning to the interpretations put on them by minor prophets. In the same way today, ministers and priests tell their people things that are not true and not even a part of their teaching; at the moment it helps them to maintain discipline. I remember one such case. A Roman Catholic priest told a couple who had been unable to attend mass one Sunday that there was no possibility of their being forgiven. They would have to be in purgatory for thousands of years for that one offense and that if it happened a second time, it would probably be totally unforgivable. He thought that this would drive them to attend mass for fear of eternal damnation. I am sure that many of the things that have come down to us in religious literature represent only a temporary interpretation by someone trying to enforce discipline, because no one of mystical enlightenment has ever taught that there is unforgivable sin.

Mysticism, which is conscious contact with God, always reveals: "Neither do I condemn thee." "Though your sins be scarlet, you will be white as snow." "I will never leave thee nor forsake thee." "God's rain falls on the just and the unjust." Everyone who has attained conscious realization of God has received this same revelation, and it is found in the teachings of all mystics.

So do not quibble about words. Do not "strain at gnats while swallowing elephants." Remember too: Not all that is published as truth is Truth. So, go within for spiritual meanings and unfoldment, and they will come to you. That is, go beyond words into the spirit.

As we turn to the within, we find solutions to our individual problems so that we do not have to steal, lie, cheat, defraud, or murder. I know all these appearances. I was part of the human world long enough to know all of its arguments. But I say, "There is no need for such solutions, because there is a withinness. Turn to the Father within, the Kingdom within." The only way I know of to do this is to close my eyes to the without (the outer appearances) and let the Father within— the Infinite, Divine, Spiritual Consciousness—reveal to me the solution to my problems or to yours. When my consciousness becomes imbued with the Divine, it has healing power, it has supplying power. As individual consciousness becomes imbued with the Divine, the human consciousness begins to fade away, and all that is left is the Divine. Ultimately, someone may come to the fullness of "that mind which was in Christ Jesus" and lift the whole world. Do not think for a minute that God is limited to providing a solution only for your little problems. That would be a sad kind of a God to worship! God can solve a problem of national import without inflating your ego. Even if the solution that would save the entire world came through you, there would be no room for the inflation of your ego. You would be merely the instrument through which the solution came.

So here you have a basic principle. Always turn to the within for the solution to a problem, whether it is a problem for you, your family, your neighbor, your patient, your student, or even if it is a national or international problem. If there is a problem of weather or epidemic in your city, if there is a national election coming up, do not be afraid to go to the Father within for the answer. Through you, the Father can answer the whole problem of a national election and will leave you more humble in spirit than ever, because you will know that you have witnessed the hand of God in action and the small part you have played. The only part we play is being willing to turn within for a solution instead of turning to books or to the intellect.

When you work with the principles of The Infinite Way as given in my 1959 and 1960 classes, you are developing your spiritual consciousness and coming into the awareness of Spirit and living in that Spirit. And when you are living in Spirit, you can say as the Master said, "What did hinder you? Pick up your bed and walk. Open your eyes."

For us in The Infinite Way two things are important. The first is that we must know the correct letter of the message of The Infinite Way so that we are not giving out part Christian Science, part Unity, part New Thought, and part Infinite Way and saying that it is all truth. It is not all truth! It is not truth to say that mind is God, because mind can be used by man, but God cannot. It is not truth to say that mind is God, because mind can be used for both good and evil, but God cannot. To even suggest that thought is power, whether it is good thought or bad thought, is far from truth. So, to present one, two, three, or four different messages and call it truth is absurd!

The correct letter of the message of The Infinite Way is certainly important, because without it you will be giving misconceptions as to what constitutes the principles of The Infinite Way. But even if you have the correct letter of truth, you have nothing unless you are so clothed in the Spirit that you can feel within yourself, "The Spirit of the Lord God is upon me, and I am ordained to speak the Truth or to heal."

That is the second important thing for us in The Infinite Way. Teachers or practitoners of The Infinite Way must never forget, not even for an hour, that the words that come through our lips constitute the least part of our teaching and healing ministry. Even when the words are the correct letter of Truth, they have no power! Only the consciousness with which the words are clothed have power! Therefore, never start your day's work without first meditating sufficiently to attain the conscious realization that you are "clothed in the Spirit" or are given some other sign to show that you realize that you yourself are not doing this work or giving this work, but that you are only the instrument through which it is coming.

It may, and often does, require two to six periods of meditation a day for the teacher or practitioner to get that assurance so that he or she does not degenerate into merely mouthing words or giving quotations or even expounding the most advanced metaphysics or mysticism. Be assured that you can read it all in books. If what comes out of your mouth has nothing more behind it than a printed page, you are giving nothing more than a printed page!

There must, of course, be an orderly procedure of study. I recommend that students start with the introduction to my book *Living the Infinite Way*, spending several days on it and then going on into the book. Then I recommend spending two or three days studying the introduction to my book *Practicing the Presence* (New York: Harper Bros., 1958), then go on into the book. Why all this time on the introduction? Because the introduction sets a foundation: the object of the book, what you are to attain, why you are to attain it, and the reason for all that follows. Reading books of this nature without knowing why or what the expected result is, is folly! You accomplish nothing unless you go into the book knowing why you are going into it and what you expect to get out of it. Then, after a few readings, you can go back to the introduction and ask yourself, "Did I get that?" If not, then you must go back again. These are not books to merely read and think that they are very sweet and nice! They are books to be worn out until a new copy is needed!

Then I recommend the student to *The Art of Meditation* (New York: Harper Bros., 1956) and *The Art of Spiritual Healing*. From there on, any of The Infinite Way books are in any order.

However, I always point out that the books *The Infinite Way Letters* of 1954, 1955, 1956, 1957, 1958, and 1959; and *Our Spiritual Resources* (New York: Harper & Row, 1960); and *The Contemplative Life* (New York: Citadel, 1976) contain in every chapter certain principles and their application. You can always go to these books and find a working tool. There is also a list of specific chapters in the above books that will give you the answers to almost every individual problem that may be brought to you. This is the way in which the books should be utilized.

I do not know at what point students will be ready for *The Thunder of Silence* (New York: Harper & Row, 1961) and *Parenthesis in Eternity*, (New York: Harper & Row, 1963), because these two books are a hundred years ahead of their time. But the only way we will grow up to them is by living in them.

In each of the Infinite Way monthly *Letters* is a lesson that is an outline for study and practice. I encourage each group to have one night a month (or one day a month) to show the students how to pick out the "pearls," how to apply them, how to use them, and how to live with them, because this is your study. The monthly *Letters* should be the study, because each provides the working principles.

To unify a study group, I recommend that a quotation be given from either the Bible or from The Infinite Way, not both. In meditation we should have one single point to concentrate and dwell upon. The purpose of using such a quotation is to center us on some specific principle.

Confidentiality of Teacher's Personal Message to an Individual Student

In India when a student reaches a certain stage of spiritual development, his teacher gives him or her a personal message. It is usually a passage of Scripture that has been given to the teacher for that specific student; except for very unusual circumstances, the master seldom gives that same passage to another student. The teacher instructs each student, "Keep this passage locked up within you. Let it be your bread, meat, wine, and water. Let it be your secret and sacred word that actually becomes the substance of your life. Never reveal this passage to anyone or you will lose it!" In turn, when the students become teachers, they impart a secret word or message to each of their students with the same warning.

This story is told in India. A master gave a disciple a secret message with the usual caution never to reveal it, saying that if he did, he would lose it. The student pondered this, then asked himself, "Why should I be so selfish? If this passage will do so much for me, imagine what it will do for all these poor people out here on the street! Why should I keep this locked up?" He promptly went to a street corner and gathered all of the people together to hear his secret message. Of course, they looked at him as if he were mad! They received nothing, and he lost what he had.

That is why we in The Infinite Way do not run around throwing our pearls before unprepared minds, even if we think they would benefit from our gems. Usually it proves to be of no value to them, and because of the world's indifference or lack of recognition, it becomes somewhat lost to us. It is like standing on a street corner showing a pearl to everybody and having them walk by as if it could have no value since we were willing to share it with everyone. A few weeks ago a man stood on a very busy street corner trying to give away dollar bills. In seven hours he was able to give away only four of them. Why is this? No one wants our treasure if we do not value it as a treasure! We must therefore be wise in speaking our pearls of wisdom.

In spiritual work, give help, insofar as possible, to those who ask for it, but do not give them the gems of your spiritual wisdom until they are prepared to receive it. As the Master, Christ Jesus, instructed us, give milk to the babies and meat only to those who are prepared for it.

It is very sad to hear a metaphysician say to the uninitiated, "Disease is not real . . . there are no accidents in Divine
Mind . . . there is no power in evil." In my opinion, metaphysi-
cians who voice such truths to the uninitiated do not actually
know these truths but are merely mouthing something they
have heard or read without having experienced it. I am sure
many of you have been given some lightly spoken message of
truth when you have been in pain or discord. And you are jus-
tified in thinking, "Well, if it's true, why didn't it work? If you
(the practitioner) know it, why aren't you helping me?"

It has been my experience that when I am asked for help,
the wisest thing I can do is say, "I will give you help. I will be
with you immediately." I say nothing more than is necessary
to convey the assurance that I will stand by with the patient
or student. Then, if I really have a consciousness of the unre-
ality of a condition, the patient responds to it. But if I try to
give them an oral message, it may even repel them. It is not
proper to go into the deep things of metaphysics with those
who are unprepared and unreceptive to them.

As you sit in class (or study my writings) even if you cannot immediately demonstrate these principles, you at least have
the feeling that they represent Truth that is coming from the
mouth of God and that the principles can be demonstrated.
Because of your background of study, you understand every word
I say to you. It makes no difference whether your background is
Christian Science or Unity or New Thought. If you have studied enough, you have been prepared and are receptive to the
message of The Infinite Way. I would not dare to say some
things to the unprepared outside of these classes. First of all,
my words could be misunderstood. Second, in being repeated by
those who do not know the nature of them, these words could
be so completely twisted as to be really dangerous.

It happened to the Master, Christ Jesus. He had no designs
on Caesar nor any desire to overthrow the Hebrew church.
But when He said that He was here on earth to establish a new

Kingdom, He was falsely quoted and His words misinterpreted, with the result that He was feared to be the enemy of Caesar and of the Hebrew church.

In my classes I often make statements about government. I would not be surprised if someone has misunderstood and received the impression that I do not like our government or would like to change it. Not at all! As far as human governments go, we have about the best there is on earth, even with all of its faults. And as far as human freedom and liberty go, we have more than any other country. So I have no complaint with our government.

Any human government is subject to change, because there is a coming and going of humans in high office and there is a coming and going of voters. Therefore, human government can be good or bad. That is all that can be expected of human government. Therefore, we must turn to Scripture, which tells us, "The government shall be on God's shoulder." Not on the Republican or Democratic or Socialist or Communist shoulder, but on His shoulder.

The function of The Infinite Way is to reveal to you the spiritual nature of your being so that your life is governed by your own state of spiritual consciousness and not by persons or conditions external to you. The degree of harmony that comes into your experience is proportionate to the degree of your own spiritual development. No one can bring about for you a demonstration greater than your own attained state of consciousness. They may do so temporarily by bringing about a healing or an opening of supply for you because they are lifting you above your attained state of consciousness. But unless you attain a higher state of consciousness of your own, you may go back to the consciousness that produced the discord in the first place and may even find that you have made room for many more discords than you had before.

The object of our work is not to find a master who will live your life for you, but rather to find a master that is your own developed consciousness and that now lives your life. Instead of believing that Jesus (or any man) is responsible for your safety, security, health, abundance, and joy, you will know that Christ *is* the substance and activity and law of your life and Christ *is* your attained state of consciousness.

Why are we subject to sin, disease, accident, poverty, and all of the horrors of human existence? Because in our human-hood we are "man of earth," and we are "that creature which is not under the law of God." In our humanhood there is no Law of God governing us. We are separate and apart from that Law. We are living as human beings, with chance, change, accident, and so on as the governing factors in our lives.

When the Spirit of God dwells in us—that is, as we attain conscious oneness with God—these sins, false appetites, and false desires drift away from us. Usually they drift away slowly, but in some cases, they go very suddenly and completely. As we come to Truth, we find that not only the ills of the body that we are aware of begin to disappear, but also many ills of the body that lie latent and undiscovered within us are likewise dispelled before they ever come to fruition. Eventually you will find that you are no longer as greatly subject to colds, flu, changing weather or climate, indigestion, or any minor claims that affect you. Gradually you will find that years go by without even a sign of anything of a discordant nature, or at least none worth mentioning. You may not be 100 percent free from any discord, but certainly you will be far freer of discord, inharmony, lack, and limitation than the world about you.

How is the transition made from being a man or woman of earth to being one who has his or her being in Christ? How do we go from being a creature who is not under the Law of God to being the Son of God—God, on whose shoulders the government rests? There are two ways.

One is by an act of Grace—of which you know nothing and for which you know no reason—whereby you suddenly become illumined and find yourself no longer of earth, no longer worldly. The pleasures and pains of human experience drop away from you. Your body does everything you expect of it, but it is no longer tired or worn out or deteriorating or full of false appetites. It no longer intrudes on your consciousness; it is there only as a vehicle. You also find yourself free of the fear of lack. You live in a consciousness that utilizes everything of this world and even enjoys the many abundances that eventually come, but without attachment, without any sense of needing, wanting, desiring. You will find a change in your human relationships, because although you enjoy all people, you do not miss any of them. Their physical presence is of less importance. These are some of the fruits of illumination, the fruits of the Christ experience. But this act of Grace comes to relatively few people in each generation.

The other way is to attain it by your own efforts. Not all men and women can attain it, only those who have been led to a spiritual teaching. You do not come to a spiritual teaching of your own free will and accord even though you may believe that your wisdom brought you here. Be assured that it is not your wisdom that brought you to this spiritual teaching. No one advertised or sent for you, just as no one advertised or sent for the others who remain outside. Most of them could be here with us; there is nothing keeping them from here. They have the same access. They are not here because the finger of God has not been placed on them.

You may believe that you have come of your own free will and accord, but the fact is that the finger of God has touched you and it is God who has pushed you into a spiritual direction. Even though you may not be aware of it, something greater than you has pushed you into this spiritual path. It is then that you can choose how many hours a day you will devote to it or what degree of effort you will make to attain the stillness and silence of meditation. You can determine whether or not you will set aside periods to practice the letter of Truth until it becomes the spirit of Truth. You can determine whether your ultimate illumination or realization will come in one year, or three, or five, or whether it will be drawn out to twenty years. Your ultimate realization and illumination is already assured because the finger of God is upon you. If the finger of God were not upon you, you would be satisfied to be working mentally to get a better automobile or better companionship or a better home. But once you have gone beyond the stage where immediate demonstration is your first consideration to where you realize that even if you never demonstrated health or supply you still could not turn back from the spiritual path, then rest assured that the rest is inevitable. But time knoweth no man; no man can tell what minute the Spark of illumination will rise in you. Sometimes I have witnessed it in students at their very first meditation with me. At other times I have witnessed their struggles over many years before they have attained it.

Some have the fanciful belief that once they have experienced spiritual illumination, their lives will be euphoric and they will be sitting on cloud nine playing a harp! It is not that way! Do not believe for a moment that gaining this moment of illumination will free you *permanently* from your discords. First of all, the greatest temptations come *after* the illumination; and second, the penalty is much more severe when an offense is committed by someone who has received spiritual illumination, because much more is expected of those who have much. The smallest offense committed by those who have attained spiritual illumination can wreck their entire careers or destroy their health or minds.

Temptation

Once we have received a touch of spiritual illumination, the penalty for succumbing to temptation is much more severe for us than it is for another who commits a serious crime. You have seen that human beings can commit many sins without suffering serious repercussions—a lie here or there, a little cheating here or there, a little false appetizing, a little stealing. With the first touch of spiritual illumination, that can never be again.

Your real temptation will come after the first illumination, although you may think such temptations are already behind you. Even the Master, Christ Jesus, was faced with three terrible temptations in the wilderness after He had become a Savior and Spiritual Master.

There are many forms of temptation: the temptation to make miracles in order to get supply, the temptation to glorify your ego, the temptation to show forth how spiritually powerful you are, and so on. Until you are faced with it, you will never know what a great temptation it is to use some human means to overcome some lack you may experience. You know very well that if you do resort to human means, your hand will fall off, because relying on human means is a form of looking back, and you may turn into a pillar of salt!

Another temptation is prosperity. Some find that as soon as they have been touched by the Light, every avenue seems to open up to fill them with abundance. They do not realize that they are being sorely tempted, more than if they were experiencing a lack. I do not have to tell you what money does to some people. You know what any kind of abundance can do in taking us from the straight and narrow path.

Health is another form of temptation. Many times I have seen people who come into a Truth teaching find really wonderful health—as if a rebirth had taken place—within a year or so. They are then tempted to coast along and make no further effort to develop a higher consciousness. They do not realize that they have not yet attained a tabernacling with the essence of their health. That is, they have not yet realized the spiritual Source of their health. Therefore the health that they enjoy today may be only the health of youth, and it may take only a touch of age to turn that health upside down.

Another temptation is the one Peter faced. Remember how Peter denied his Master? He made his life, his freedom, and his security dependent on a lie. In doing so, he denied the very spiritual Source of all freedom. Fortunately, he awakened in time; Judas Iscariot did not. Selling one's birthright for thirty pieces of silver is equivalent to selling our spiritual consciousness for the sake of something in the world of effect, whether it is freedom or something else.

Temptations come in many forms to turn us back to the consciousness we have outgrown. But we can no longer depend on material and human sources and resources. So let us not succumb to human temptation. Whatever form of temptation comes to you, recognize it for what it is and it will pass by.

Spiritual Activity Is Self-Perpetuating

When you are called into an activity of this kind, you will be called upon to do healing work. But beware of building a practice or a student body by man-made means, because you will have to build a wall around it to protect it and nothing is more destructive than a sense of competition.

You will not have to protect a spiritually built practice or student body because the consciousness that drew these people to you will maintain and sustain it. Whatever is of God is Self-maintained and Self-sustained. If you realize that, you will not lose faith and you will not be afraid of losing your practice or your student body. You will not fear competition.

So do not try to hold on to individual patients or students, because your good does not flow from clients, patients, or students. Be perfectly willing to let patients and students come and go, because they do so according to their consciousness. Trying to hold on to individual patients or students will not perpetuate your practice or student body or church. It is an attempt to perpetuate human beings and their checkbooks. Always be willing to let your patients go if they are drawn to another practitioner or teacher, and rejoice that they have found someone else who represents their state of consciousness.

I let those who are led of the Spirit come to me. If for some reason they are led in another direction, it is my greatest joy that they have found the state of consciousness that best meets their need. It makes no difference to me whether it is within The Infinite Way or outside of it. I have been careful to not in any way proselyte or encourage anyone in Christian Science, Unity, New Thought, or any other activity to leave their activities to come into this work. I myself would hesitate to humanly encourage a single soul to step out of their own orbit. What they do through divine guidance is another thing.

The edifice I have built is a spiritual one, because it was a divine unfoldment, and each year it is maintained and sustained by something inherent in its nature. I have no fear that anyone now or in the future will ever succeed in interfering with it, because it has no human entanglements. I was given that assurance some time ago when I was concerned that some of our students were forcefully attempting to organize The Infinite Way. Although I knew they could not succeed while I was around, I was concerned about what they would do when I was no longer around. I took it into meditation, and very clearly the Father spoke, "The Infinite Way is a spiritual creation, and that which sent it into human consciousness will maintain and sustain it," and God help those who try to interfere!

And so it is with your individual activity. If you spiritually build a practice or student body, the consciousness that drew it to you will maintain it and sustain it. Your spiritual church will not be invaded.

Consciousness of Truth

Healing work is a matter of a state of consciousness. It is not a question of knowledge. If a correct teaching were the only thing necessary for healing work, all you would have to do is learn The Infinite Way books and set out to be a healer. But do not fool yourself about that! You must go far beyond learning what is in the books; you have to develop an actual consciousness.

Thousands of students of New Thought have been graduated and have been licensed as practitioners, yet few have been able to heal. The tragedy is in thinking that you can take a course of lessons and learn some truth you can declare and that this will make you a healer. That is utter nonsense! I have had students go through a dozen classes with me, and they cannot heal. On the other hand, I have had some students go through only one class and do fine healing work. But those students had already developed a consciousness and were prepared for it. I have seen the same thing happen to students of other approaches to Truth. So it isn't the courses that help you to heal. It is your consciousness.

We do not need words or thoughts in living or in healing work. The fewer words and thoughts we use in dealing with our patients, the better, because very often words antagonize and interfere with the healing. When I am called on for help, I avoid voicing Truth and merely give the assurance, "I will help you." If I am not feeling well or if I need some other kind of help, I very happily turn to some of my students. If they start voicing Truth to me, I resent it very much, because I am not interested in what they think or know about Truth or what they think I ought to know about Truth. What I want is *consciousness* of Truth, and I do not like hearing statements that have more or less become clichés. So when you are asked for help, give as great assurance as possible that you are standing by, not with words, clichés, or mere lip service but with a real consciousness of the Presence.

There are some who fool themselves into believing that they have attained a consciousness of God's Presence, but they have not attained it at all! How can you tell? By the fruitage in your life experience! If you find that there is a Presence going before you to make the crooked places straight, if you are experiencing a continuous harmony, if your problems are being solved quickly and easily, there is no question that you have attained a consciousness of God's Presence.

But if you are continuously running into problems that do not solve themselves or do not quickly disappear, you may be fooling yourself. You may be having only an emotional jag! This happens too often in the metaphysical world, especially to emotional people. They have some kind of emotional experience, or a sensation of some kind, and believe that they have the realization of God's Presence. That is not a good foundation! You can tell by the fruitage in your life whether you have the realization of God's Presence. If the problems of your life and of those who appeal to you for help are being met, you have the Presence. But if not, then go a step further and see if you can really attain that Presence that announces *Itself* by fruitage. If you are consciously one with God, you will know it by the spiritual fruitage in your life.

Everything that takes place in your life is the result of something in consciousness. There is no external event without an internal cause. Always remember that there are no outer things taking place except what can be accounted for within. It is this inner change in your consciousness that is productive of the harmony in your outer experience. An inner love, an inner mellowness, becomes evident as outer harmonious relationships.

A mystic is one who attains conscious union with God, and mystics never die. Once they have attained conscious union with God, they cannot die. Such mystics as Abraham, Isaac, Jacob, Moses, Elijah, Elisha, Isaiah, Joel, Naomi, Jesus,

John, Paul, Lao Tsu, Buddha, and Shankara merely pass from
the human scene in order to be able to do their work better
than they could on the human plane, and the work of the mystics continues. So from behind the human scene, we have had
for thousands of years the cumulative work of these mystics
pouring into our consciousness. It is through these mystics that
we receive the spiritual impulses that turn us toward mystical or
religious teachings, toward God. By their spiritual oneness with
God, they are drawing us into their orbit. But they can draw
into their orbit only those who are receptive and responsive.

As you go along, you will find that you will be able to draw
into your orbit only those who are receptive and responsive to
an urge for God. Many times you will be hurt, because you cannot draw members of your own family unless they are receptive.
At the same time, you will find an utter stranger being drawn
almost instantly into your circle, and you will wonder, "Why
couldn't this have been my husband or my child or my parent
or my sister or brother?" It cannot be! We cannot choose those
who are to come into our circle. All we can do is live in our
conscious union with God and let those who are ready for the
experience be attracted to us.

We cannot go to the world and tell it to be spiritual. We
cannot go before an audience and say, "Wouldn't you like to
be spiritual?" They are not interested in it, and they would
laugh in our faces. Why should they want to be spiritual? The
only possible success is by admitting the Christ into consciousness. The only contribution we can make to the world is to
admit the Christ into their consciousness and create in them a
hunger, a thirst, for spiritual righteousness.

I originally discovered that when the Spirit of the Lord was
upon me, my patients and my students had their healings, had
their desire for spirituality, had their upliftment. But when I did
not have It, then I could not create that desire in them, because nothing that I humanly said could do it. But when the
Spirit is upon me, I do not even have to talk. I do not even

have to teach. I do nothing but sit in meditation and prayer, and those who come to me have a greater desire for the Christ, a greater thirst for righteousness, because when the Spirit of the Lord God is upon me, *It* touches them.

So it will be with you! When the Spirit of the Lord God is upon you, you are then appointed to comfort those who mourn, heal those who are sick, raise the dead, and reform the sinner. But you do not do it; you do not even know when it happens. Many times you will be shocked by someone saying to you, "Do you know that the few minutes we spent together had a wonderful effect on me?" Well, you had nothing to do with it as far as your conscious direction of thought was concerned. But you had everything to do with it in that through meditation you were filled with the Spirit.

This Spirit of the Lord God that is upon you is "a sword unto every form of discord there is." That is why the Master said, "I come not to bring peace, but a sword." When those who are materialistic and want to hold on to their discords feel the prick of that sword, they will sometimes turn on you and rend you because they feel that you are exposing their very faults and that you are tearing from them the very thing that gives them their happiness or their profits. You are not, of course, because you know nothing about their faults or what brings them happiness or profit. But they feel naked in your presence, and that is how they feel.

Please remember that as students of The Infinite Way, we owe a debt to this world, a debt that we can repay only if we can bring the Spirit of the Lord God into its consciousness, the Spirit that heals, saves, redeems, reforms, enriches. If we can live morning, noon, and night so as to be fully aware of the Christ Spirit within us, we will bless all those who are receptive and responsive to Truth and who come into our orbit.

We cannot help everyone, because not all want it in this way. There are those who want only loaves and fishes, silver and gold, and they will very frankly tell you that that is all they want. Some do not even know that it is all they want. You must not be discouraged if you are not helping everyone in the world or even everyone who comes to you, because some will want only the *result* of what you have but will not want to take what you have along with it. No one in our present day is healing everybody or reforming everybody or bringing the Christ to everybody. We cannot be concerned with everybody! Our only concern is to stay as filled with the Spirit as we can and then let *It* reach where *It* will. If *It* reaches only one person in this room, that is not my responsibility; it is yours. If *It* reaches everyone, I am grateful. But it is not my fault if *It* does not reach everybody. My only responsibility is to live consciously in oneness with the Father. The degree of benefit you receive depends on what use you make of it after I have done my part. The student who gives hours of study, meditation, thought, and prayer to the message I am giving you will gain ten times more than the student who says, "Well, that was a beautiful class," and then returns to the human way of living. But that is not my responsibility; it is yours.

And so it is with you. You are responsible only for the degree of Christliness you embody within yourself. You are responsible for the amount of study, prayer, and meditation you devote to the realization of Christhood. Then you will share it freely with those who come to you, because you cannot help it. But the degree that they benefit will depend upon their own ability to forsake the world.

The disciples Paul, Peter, and John were not to blame because Demas, after accompanying them and working with them for years on their missionary tours, went back to the ways of the world. The disciples were not at fault; it was Demas's degree of inability to forsake the world; he loved the world better than the Spirit. In the same way, you cannot blame the Master because Judas went astray. The Master had done His work with all the disciples, but there remained in Judas a trace of desire for the world's goods, whether it was fame, position, or place.

Everyone who has been a spiritual teacher has found that there are students who in the end betrayed them, no matter how much was given to them. The Master had it happen to Him, as did Peter and Paul. In our modern day, some of Mrs. Eddy's top students deserted her, as did Mrs. Fillmore's. Everyone has found it so. It cannot be avoided, and it is no use grieving about it. It happens because, in some form or another, the world is too attractive to them. With some, it is glory; with others, it is money. Whatever its form, it is the world. No matter how close they get to the Throne, there will be some who in the end will desert you or in some way attempt to cheat you and defraud you. They only defraud themselves and throw themselves right out of the spiritual work!

But that is not your responsibility. Your responsibility is living in conscious union with God, staying in the Spirit, and then sharing it to the greatest extent you can with those who come to you. Those who can benefit—those who can leave the world—will go to the top. Others will benefit in proportion to their ability to accept it. Others will derive no benefit at all. But that will not be your fault!

Healing Work

In this work we find there are claims that will not yield to a practitioner working on the mental level but that do yield to a practitioner working on the spiritual level. In other words, there are people whom medicine just does not seem to benefit, yet these people respond very well to a mental practitioner. Others do not respond to mental treatment but will respond very quickly when they find a practitioner who works on the spiritual plane. Who are the spiritually minded practitioners who work only on the spiritual plane? I have not found many. Almost all metaphysical practice is on the mental plane, with a little of spiritual touching it. But there are some who work only on the spiritual plane, and finding them is a matter of demonstration. We must go within and ultimately be led to the practitioner who can meet our need.

Sometimes even the practitioner on the spiritual plane will fail to meet certain cases. The practitioner may not at the moment be on a high enough level of spirituality, or the patient may not yet be ready to yield—that is, may not be ready to give up the nets, or the physical sense of existence. As an example, a woman in Boston had the very finest practitioners and the very finest teachers. But for nine years she did not get a healing. She finally came to the realization that there was no hope and that she was dying. The thought came to her, "Well, I guess I'm just one of these who do not respond. I may was well give up trying to be healed. I'll spend these last weeks or months trying to find God. When I pass, I'll at least have a better opportunity of coming into God's presence." The next day she awoke healed. As soon as she gave up the effort to be healed and sought God, she was healed. Why is this? Well, for those nine years she had been violating the law of Spirit, which says, "Take no thought for your little life or what ye shall eat, or what ye shall drink, or wherewithal ye shall be clothed. Your heavenly Father knoweth what things ye have need of, and it is His good pleasure to give you the Kingdom. Seek ye the Kingdom of God, and all these things will be answered." Very few people come to a practitioner seeking God. Most come to a practitioner seeking a healing or seeking supply—something *from* God. On the spiritual level this cannot be done. Therefore, when a patient clings to his physical sense of existence, healing cannot take place.

Materia medica does great work on the material or physical plane. You might also take a claim to a mental practitioner and have it met. But all the mental practitioner does is substitute a belief of health for the belief of sickness. In other words, the mental practitioner changes the patient who is under the belief of being sick into a person who is under the belief of being well. Why is it only a belief of being well? Because it is subject to change again!

When you come to a spiritual practitioner—a practitioner of the Soul or the Spirit—and ask, "Can you get God to do this for me (heal my body, heal my pocketbook, heal my unemployment)?" the practitioner who knows the Spirit says, "No, I am sorry but I haven't such an influence with God. I can bring God to you, if you are interested." By that time, many patients pack up their bags and move on, saying "Oh, I thought God would do something!"

I do not have to tell you that many people cannot, even if they would, release themselves from the desire of person, place, or thing. You would have to see my mail for a few days to realize how many people are trying to either get a companion or get rid of one! You would be surprised how many people, even after reading The Infinite Way writings for years, still write to me for a healing of a physical claim. In other words, they are still approaching God from a physical standpoint, expecting God to do something on a physical level.

We must stop thinking in terms of demonstration on the physical level and come into the consciousness of the Presence of God and demonstrate God's presence. When you come into the presence of God, I can assure you that you will never find lack, limitation, injustice, sin, disease, or death, because none of these things exist in the Presence of God. You cannot have health, wealth, success, or happiness separate and apart from God. If you desire God, you find your health, your wealth, your success embodied in God.

Most of the responsibility for healing is on the practitioner because the practitioner has to live so high in consciousness that nearly everything responds to his or her work. Then it is up to the patients. If they do not turn to the Spirit and begin to unfold in spiritual development, they have no cause for complaint if healing does not take place. However, in our work we never sit in judgment as to whether or not a person deserves a healing. We never say, "It is your fault." When a person comes to us with a problem, we undertake it with the understanding that if we can rise high enough in consciousness, the need will be met, although not necessarily at that particular moment. Sometimes a delay is even better!

One woman came to me for help in selling her house. It was worth much more than she was willing to accept. We worked on the problem for an entire month, but the house was not sold. Six months later we worked on the problem for another month. She said, "I don't understand it. You have such a reputation for successful work, and yet it has failed in this case." I asked her how she knew the work had failed." She replied, "Well, the house hasn't been sold." I said, "Well, I'm not a real estate agent. I was praying for a realization of God and for God's guidance. Anything could come out of that. For all I know, selling the house might be the wrong thing." Less than a year later she sold her house for the full market value, and during that time she was saved from making an unwise investment that would have resulted in her losing whatever money she would have realized from the sale of her house at the lower price.

In my own student days, many of my problems were not being met when I went to practitioners. In those days all I was seeking was to have my nets filled with fish. I was seeking harmony of body, of mind, of business. If my problems had been met one after another, what incentive would I have had to search deeper? Whatever is happening through me today may be traced back to those early failures, because they made me determined to study more and learn more about the Truth of Being.

Kate Buck (who sought a healing for nine years) was a young woman when she was healed and had sixty years as a wonderful practitioner. But it took nine years for her to come to the realization that God *is*.

Many of you, I am sure, while studying whatever form of Truth you have been following, have had healings for which no specific work was done. When your mind was not on the specific healing, the healing took place. I had many such experiences in my early years. Just studying and reading, I found problems falling away from me without any specific treatment. Why? Because I was not seeking a healing; I was seeking Truth in those books, and the healings came of their own accord.

To the degree that we stop seeking greater harmony and seek only a realization of God, we will find discord disappearing. But remember that many, if not most, of our problems have to do with our attachments. We are still carrying the burden of the lack of demonstration on the part of our spouses, children, parents, relatives, friends, or business associates, and we will carry that burden as long as we have those ties. Let us not complain too bitterly about those problems but continue to work until they are all solved.

Start with the realization that it is your conscious union with God that makes your demonstration. It makes no difference whether we do no business today or have no patients or students today or no income today. Our conscious union with God in some way meets our needs. Scripture gives us many examples. Moses had no income, but manna fell from the sky. Elijah had no congregation, but he found cakes baked on the stones. The widow who shared her mite had a cruse of oil that never ran dry. And Jesus multiplied loaves and fishes. As long as you have your conscious union with God, your demonstration is assured.

CHAPTER 9

FREEDOM IN GOD

Some nations seek political freedom—freedom from dictators and concentration camps. Other nations seek freedom from religious bondage—from teachings that hold them in bondage and make them slaves of men rather than servants of God.

Any nation that has gained political, economic, or religious freedom has had to fight hard to attain that freedom and must work even harder to retain it, because there are those who would take that freedom away. There is not one moment of the day when someone, somewhere, is not plotting to control the minds and bodies of individuals, to control nations and the world itself. Not all the enemies are in foreign countries; some can be found within a country itself.

The freedom we seek is a spiritual freedom—a freedom in Christ, in God. It is not a freedom from anyone or some circumstance or some condition of lack, limitation, sin, or disease—although we may have started out seeking only that kind of freedom.

Spiritual Freedom

Spiritual freedom is a freedom attained *in* God. There is no such thing as freedom *from* anything or anyone. The longer we attempt to gain freedom *from* sin, disease, death, lack, or limitation, the more we are kept in bondage to such conditions. What we must seek is freedom *in* God, *in* Christ—a spiritual freedom.

Originally, we were given spiritual freedom as a divine inheritance, but there was an experience in consciousness called "the fall of man" or the "prodigal experience" in which we set up a selfhood apart from God. We thereby lost our divine inheritance, and spiritual freedom is no longer something that is given to us. Now we must struggle to regain our spiritual freedom. We cannot regain it until we return to the state of consciousness we call oneness, unity, or union with God. Like the prodigal son, we must return to the Father's house.

Our spiritual freedom is not gained through the efforts of others. The efforts of others can only instruct us and give us a little wisdom. Throughout the ages there have been saviors, saints, sages, seers, prophets, and great "literary lights" who attained spiritual wisdom. Through their teachings and their writings, we have been given the benefit of their soul suffering and physical suffering. They pay the price in physical suffering and soul suffering to bring forth a spiritual truth, which we sometimes regard so lightly. To receive the benefit of their light, we must pay the price in effort and devotion in the degree that we desire spiritual freedom. You must know the Truth to attain spiritual freedom in God, in Christ.

Having regained our spiritual freedom, we must continue to work hard in order to retain it, because spiritually within us we have enemies of our own household, within our own consciousness, within our very being. They are the enemies who would put us to sleep with the idea that someone can come out of the sky, wave a magic wand, and set us free, with no effort on our part. We must work hard constantly to protect ourselves from accepting such universal beliefs and superstitions.

Those who receive spiritual illumination find that they no longer have problems of their own. First of all, illumination changes their desires and needs and simplifies them to the extent that they need so little of this world's good that never again do they have a problem of supply. What little they do require appears when necessary in miraculous ways. They have no economic problems for themselves or physical, mental, or moral problems. That one touch of illumination removes those persons from the world.

As you receive some measure of illumination, you too will have very little to meet in the way of problems. But you will find a problem that has its basis in your husband, your wife, your child, your mother or father, your mother-in-law, or your business. You will not want your employees to be unemployed, so you play God to your employees. Or you will have to maintain a home for your in-laws or your children or your grandchildren, and you will take upon yourself their demonstration and the solution of their problems. Look back in your experience and see how you would have had fewer problems if there had been no family, relatives, or friends whom you had to consider. Most of our problems arise because we cannot live our own lives in accordance with our own understanding and our own demonstration of our Christhood. Why? Because we have to consider those who are not ready for their demonstration, and we are not yet ready to leave mother, father, brother, or sister.

Just recently I was struck by the significance of the Bible passage, "Leave your nets, and follow me." Out of that experience has come my booklet *Leave Your Nets*. When Jesus said to his disciples, "Follow me," they left their nets and their families and followed Him. They no longer looked to the Christ to fill their nets. They left their nets, left all of their human sense of good and supply, left their families. We find no record that their families suffered from being left. Evidently their problems of supply were over. Their fulfillment came in some other way.

Watch this carefully in your experience. When a problem of any nature arises, trace it back, and you will see that it really is not your problem at all. It is one that has been placed upon you by virtue of a family relationship or some other. This is how you will benefit from it. Once you recognize a problem is not yours, the problem is three-quarters on its way to being solved. The difficulty comes from your claiming it as "my problem." It is the word *my* that blocks us from the unfoldment of the solution. Come to a place of realizing that it really is not your problem at all, and you will see how soon the solution comes.

The illumined individual has no economic, physical, mental, or moral problems. That one touch of the Spirit removes you from the world. Then what happens? Instead of retiring from the world and enjoying the fruits of the Spirit, you feel compelled to go out to try to save the world, and from then on you take on the burdens of the world. This results in expenses, and you form an organization to raise money. Eventually you come to the realization, "Why am I having this problem? I can't benefit from this. I don't need it." Then you say, "The world needs it!"

All this has been known. Paul wrote to the Philippians, "What I choose I know not, for I am in a strait betwixt two—having a desire to depart and be with Christ which is far better, [and a desire] to abide in the flesh [which] is more needful for you. . . . I shall abide . . . with you for your furtherance and joy of faith." So for their sakes, Paul remained to teach and ended up in jail. The same thing happened to John. Even the Master Christ Jesus ended up on the cross. Why was He crucified? Because His teachings were not authorized by the church. He could have retired to the hills and lived there quietly, but

He remained to teach us for your sake and mine. As Mrs. Eddy said, "If Jesus had never taken a student, He would not have been crucified."

World Work

In 1950 I was told that I was to be given a new and higher work, but it was not until the middle of January 1956 that I was told, "Begin this new and higher work." I immediately called together the six students in Hawaii who, by virtue of their being around me, were the closest to me and were receiving the most instruction and were doing the most work in The Infinite Way. We began this work. From there I went to New York City, where we were joined by thirty-three students who were leading tape-study groups. They came from all over the United States and Canada, and three times a week the thirty-three met in my room, and the work was continued. From there I went to London and Manchester and finally to Australia to explain this new work. It will bring you greater blessings than you have ever known.

The Infinite Way principle of prayer and of supply is that you cannot pray to God for something to be added to you, since you are already the fullness and the completeness of God made manifest and all that the Father has is yours. You must acknowledge this and begin to open out so that the flow of God can go through you to this world that does not yet know this Truth. My mission, then, is to ask of you three periods of meditation every day for the world. These three periods of meditation are in addition to your periods of meditation for yourself, your family, your patients, and your students. These are three periods of meditation that you as part of The Infinite Way offer to me for the world.

I seek nothing for myself. Ever since the realization was given to me, I have needed nothing of man. Everything I have needed has come by Grace, and it continues to come by Grace. All that the students contribute goes back into this work in one way or another—for travel expenses, for books, and so on. So I ask nothing of you for myself, but I ask of you these periods of meditation for the world.

The world will not be reformed from outside. It will not be given peace by any treaties or by any combination of powers. The world powers will not establish peace by uniting and forming armies and navies. Armies do not establish peace; they establish wars. Navies have never maintained peace; they maintain wars. Neither will the League of Nations or the United Nations give peace to the world for the reason that they are formed for selfish purposes. You can be assured that a nation's representatives are trying to get something for their own country, not for any other country. These representatives do not really seek benefits for the world but for their own nations, and they seek it from other nations. This must always be true in the human world. In the material world, getting is the purpose in life.

It is only in the spiritual realm that we meet to give rather than to get. It has always been the religious leaders that have given to the world whatever benefits there are, such spiritual leaders as Abraham, Moses, Isaac, Jacob, Elijah, Elisha, Isaiah, Jesus, Paul, John. In this age, it will be the spiritually minded people who will save the world, because we have now rediscovered a form of prayer. It is the same form of prayer that has brought to The Infinite Way the success it has had. It enabled a lone individual to bring forth a teaching that in ten years has spread around the world, without an organization, without financing, without advertising.

In the first years of my practice, I discovered that treatments do not heal and that without treatment far better healing work resulted. One day I was talking to a woman in my office when a telephone call came from a patient suffering from excruciating pains in her head. The woman in my office, having heard the urgency of the patient on the phone, said to me, "I will leave you to take care of your patient." As I was escorting her to the door, the patient called again to tell me that the pain had gone instantaneously. I had not yet even started her treatment! Another time, a man who was dying of tuberculosis came to me for help at the urging of his office staff. I said to him, "I'll be glad to help you. Just let me take over and see what I can do for you." He replied that since I was treating him for tuberculosis, he also needed help for pyhorrea, which prevented him from eating or brushing his teeth. After he left, I started treatment for the tuberculosis and completely forgot the pyhorrea. The next morning he phoned to tell me that his teeth were so solid that he had brushed them for five minutes and they had not moved. We also had a beautiful healing of the tuberculosis. But the significant thing is that there was a perfect and complete healing of the pyhorrea, without a treatment for it.

The Secret of the Spirit

After a succession of such incidences, I was driven closer to prayer until I discovered the secret that has given us The Infinite Way. The secret is that where the Spirit of the Lord is, there is freedom, there is health, there is wholeness, there is supply, there is peace, joy, and dominion. So the secret is not to treat anyone for disease, but to attain the consciousness of God's Presence. As Jesus said, "When the Spirit of the Lord God is upon me, the mourners are comforted, the sick are healed, and the dead are raised." When the Spirit of the Lord God is upon me, Divine Grace is touching you and freedom is taking place within you. If the Spirit of the Lord God is *not* upon me, nothing happens—there is a void, a vacuum!

So, when you call upon me for help, I do not concern myself with your discords. I am not interested as to whether your trouble is physical, mental, moral, or financial. I concern myself only with attaining a conscious awareness, a feeling, of God's Presence. If I can attain that awareness, you feel it and it takes effect in you. Your whole nature—your body, your mind, your finances—responds.

Meditation: Your Gift to the World

When the Spirit of the Lord God is upon you, anyone who is reaching out to you for help receives it. If you were to attain this realization three, four, or five times a day, you would always be in some degree in the Spirit. You would never be entirely out of the Spirit. So for the sake of your own individual lives, for your patients or students, for your family, for all those who look to you for comfort, bring yourself to a conscious realization of God's Presence.

In addition, for the sake of the world, give us three periods out of every twenty-four hours in which you forget yourself, your family, your patients, your students. This is your contribution to the world. Remember that you already have "all that the Father has" and therefore you are infinite and no good can come to you. But you must open out a way for the "imprisoned splendor" to escape. Three times a day, open out a way for the Spirit of the Lord God, which is upon you, to escape out into the world.

In the first of these meditations, just meditate until you feel a consciousness of God's Presence. That is the end of the first meditation for the world. In your second meditation, after you feel this Presence, make the declaration, "This realization of Christ is dispelling material sense." In your third meditation for the world, first attain your realization of the Christ, then realize, "This realization of the Christ is opening human consciousness to the receptivity of Truth." That is all. That is your prayer. That is your gift to the world.

What is happening is that you are admitting the Christ into human consciousness three times a day. These three periods a day are your world work. The rest of the time, have this realization of the Spirit for any purpose you like—yourself, your patients, your students, your family. But reserve three periods a day for the world.

As I said earlier, we cannot go to the world and tell it to be spiritual, because people are not interested in that. But by our three periods of meditation a day for the world, the Christ will enter their consciousness and make them *want* to be spiritual. They will become as we are at this moment. We want to be spiritual. We are not really giving as full expression to the Christ as we would like to. We are not as spiritual as we would like to be. That is why we are not as happy as we could be. We know how far we are failing in being as spiritual as we would like to be, but we have the desire, the hunger, to be fully spiritual, and that is what we are doing for the world. That is the only contribution we can make to the world.